YOUR DEATH WARRANT?

Your Death Warrant?

The implications of euthanasia
A medical, legal and ethical study

Edited by
JONATHAN GOULD AND LORD CRAIGMYLE

ARLINGTON HOUSE   *New Rochelle, New York*

Contents

Note on authors

In the summer of 1968 a Study Group on Euthanasia was set up as a joint venture by the Catholic Union of Great Britain and the Guild of St Luke, Ss Cosmas and Damian (the Guild of Catholic doctors). This book is the outcome of their studies. The group was composed of the following members:

CICELY CLARKE, MA, MB, ChB, DCH, a senior medical officer in community care including geriatrics in the public health service; immediate past President of National Board of Catholic Women, a member of the Medical Women's Federation, of the British Medical Association, and of the Society of Medical Officers of Health.

LORD CRAIGMYLE, MA (Oxon), Secretary of the Catholic Union of Great Britain.

CHARLES DENT, FRS, Professor of human metabolism at University College Hospital Medical School. (A member of the Joint Study Group in its early stages only.)

J. G. FROST, MB, BCh, BAO, a general practitioner; Honorary Secretary of the Guild of St Luke, Ss Cosmas and Damian; editor of *Catholic Medical Quarterly*; recently completed work on the BMA panel set up to consider BMA views on euthanasia.

J. E. McA. GLANCY, MD, FRCP, DPM, consultant psychiatrist and physician superintendant at Goodmayes Hospital, Ilford, Essex; a member of British Medical Association, the Royal Medico-Psychological Association; Master of the Guild of St Luke, Ss Cosmas and Damian.

JONATHAN GOULD, BSc, MBBS, DPM, MRCP, a psychiatrist; has made contributions on the psychology of major crime, including murder, and alcoholism; has written on matters of general interest in psychiatry, including the physiological contribution to the treatment of mental illness; Chairman of the UK Study Group of the World Federation of Mental Health, which published *The Prevention of Damaging Stress in Children*; is author of over thirty papers which have appeared in professional journals.

F. J. HEBBERT, MD, FRCP(Glasgow), ERD, consultant physician in geriatrics at Whippscross, Langthorne and Chingord Hospitals in Essex.

JOSEPH MOLONY, KCVO, QC, a member of the Bar Council; Recorder of Bristol; Attorney General of the Duchy of Cornwall since 1960; chairman of the Board of Trade Committee on Consumer Protection in 1959, and of the Code of Practice Committee of Association of the British Pharmaceutical Industry in 1967.

G. E. MORIARTY, a barrister at law.

R. A. G. O'BRIEN, a partner in a London firm of solicitors; a member of the Solicitors' European Group; clerk of the Ward of Coleman St in the City of London; Liveryman of the City of London Solicitors' Company.

K. F. M. POLE, KHS, LRCP(Edinburgh), LRCS(Edinburgh), LRFP(Glasgow), LRFS(Glasgow), MRCGP, MD(Vienna), a general practitioner and Divisional Police Surgeon for the Kent County Constabulary; a founder-member of the Royal College of General Practitioners; author of several books and many articles.

HUGH ROSSI, MP, Conservative MP for Hornsey, a solicitor. (He retired from the Joint Study Group on being appointed an assistant Government Whip.)

P. S. TWEEDY, consultant in geriatric medicine, Stockport and Buxton Hospital Management Committee, Stockport, Cheshire.

WILLIAM T. WELLS, QC, MP, Labour MP for Walsall North; recorder of Kings Lynn; deputy chairman of the Hertfordshire Quarter Sessions; author of *How English Law Works* (Sampson Low); legal editor of *Encyclopedia Brittanica*.

TO

THOSE WHO ARE AT RISK

Acknowledgements

The members of this study group wish to thank their many friends and acquaintances who have helped them in their work, and in particular Mr Eric Goldschmid, Mrs Ginnett, Mrs Graham Hodgson and Miss Mary Roberts.

Preface

It is a great mistake to let people know that moral issues involve religion. If you talk about religion you might just as well talk about politics. Everyone agrees that politics and religion are a matter of opinion. You can take your pick. If you happen to be a religious type you take notice of what your Church approves or condemns. Otherwise you take no notice.

Let this be clear. When we talk about moral problems we are not talking about religious beliefs—which we can take or leave. Stealing, lying, killing, fornicating would be wrong even if no church condemned them. Hijacking aircraft, tossing bombs into crowded shopping centres and selling drugs to your children are not sins mentioned in the bible. Nor is euthanasia. So keep religion out of this. Just read about this plan to kill you and anyone else who becomes old or incurably sick. This book happens to contain the teaching of the Church but the Catholic Church also forbids the destruction of the unborn child so it must be rather old fashioned. This book, on the contrary, is right up-to-date. It is worth reading. If enough people read it thousands of lives will be saved. Yours, perhaps, among them.

✠ John Card. Heenan

16 February 1971 Archbishop of Westminster

Chapter I

Introduction

Why this book has been written

Euthanasia—a happy death—is every man's hope. Though we pray to be saved from sudden death, we certainly do not wish a lingering one: an easy death, in sleep perhaps, when we are already mentally and morally prepared for it—that is what most of us would ask for ourselves. When we are ill we expect our doctors to relieve us in our pain, and console us in our anxieties; in addition, a dying man expects his doctor to use his skill to make death when it comes as easy and painless as possible. In this we are seldom disappointed. If this, the literal meaning, were all that was meant by the use of the word euthanasia, there would be no one who could object to it on any grounds, nor would there be anyone who thought it necessary to pass an Act of Parliament to legalise it. It would simply be a word to describe every man's wish, and every doctor's endeavour at the approach of death. However, there is another usage of the word, coined comparatively recently and now common currency, which expresses a very different thing: in this sense euthanasia means the painless killing of men and women to end their sufferings. This one may call the morbid sense of the word—though it is frequently misleadingly called 'mercy killing'.

This book is about euthanasia in that sense, and in this book the word will only be used in that sense, unless the context indicates that the literal sense is intended. It is important, in this subject as in any other, to be quite clear about the meaning of terms: it is because the word euthanasia originally indicated something desirable that its use in another sense can so easily mislead, for more than a trace of the good odour of the word continues to hang about it.

Just as there is some confusion over the meaning of the word euthanasia, so there is confusion about the circumstances and procedures which can properly be described as euthanasia. If a doctor, in order to relieve severe pain in a patient, increases the doses of pain-killing drugs, he may incidentally hasten death : some people class this as euthanasia on the assumption that what the doctor has done amounts to 'mercy killing'. The law does not class it as killing (as is explained in Chapter V). Or, a doctor may decline to use resuscitatory techniques and allow a patient to die quickly and naturally; some people class this as 'mercy killing', but again the law does not. And the law is no ass, for in neither of these cases is the doctor actually and deliberately *killing* his patient.

From this confusion arises the idea, quite commonly heard, but quite erroneous, that a certain amount of euthanasia—in the morbid sense—is already practised. For the purpose of the current controversy the most convenient way of securing that when the term euthanasia is used it shall have an exact meaning clearly understood—thus avoiding false reasoning—is to confine it to meaning *those techniques and procedures deliberately intended to interrupt the patient's ability to sustain life, to legalise which an Act of Parliament would be necessary.* In this book therefore we shall not describe as euthanasia any procedure which is at present legal, or which is accepted without dispute as being ethically sound medical practice.

Let us be clear too that there is no discordance at the present time between what is ethically sound medical practice and what is legal. This is more fully discussed in Chapter V : suffice here to say that any doctor who is worried about the legality of a procedure he proposes to use has sound advice readily available to him, and no body of medical opinion exists which seeks to change, or even feels a need to define by declaratory statute, the law on matters touching medical procedures for the dying.

The authors' purpose in writing this book arises from the need to alert and inform public opinion about the dangers to society of legislation to permit euthanasia. Such legislation is now being stridently urged in some quarters. We attempt to show the objections to euthanasia on medical, social, legal and ethical grounds, as well as giving an account of measures which have been put forward from time to time to legalise euthanasia, with particular reference to this country.

The reasons why euthanasia is currently being mooted are not far to seek. First, the advances in the technical skill of the medical profession have enabled doctors and nurses to prevent, in many cases, the full appearances of all the conditions enabling a doctor to certify death (such as, among other things, cessation of breathing and the fall of blood pressure to zero) when in fact the body has lost for ever its *natural* power to sustain life. Now it is quite incorrect to assume that doctors are under any technical or legal obligation to continue to use all the available techniques in such circumstances; the accepted aim of medical practice is to ease the suffering of the incurably ill patient as much as possible, but not to continue to sustain life in what has been described as 'a vegetative condition'.

Secondly, at the same time as these advances have been made in medical practice, there has been a decrease in the awe in which human life is held. Much play is made of a supposed distinction between the quality of life and the quantity of life. These are terms having a certain emotive appeal and for that reason they can be used to score debating points, but they appear to have no clear definitions and to be therefore of the most limited usefulness in serious discussion. Moreover, those who use this phrase 'the quality of life' are often just those who are content to compare human and animal life on equal or almost equal terms, saying that the mercy shown to a suffering horse should be shown to a suffering human being. In this they demonstrate their lack of perception of the particular nature of the quality of human life, that mystery which is mankind.

All the authors of this book are practising members of the Roman Catholic Church. Some readers may wonder what such a group has to offer to the general public, consisting as it does

17

only to a small extent of their fellow Roman Catholics, and to a rather larger extent of Christians of other denominations and those of other religions, but mainly of those of no particular religious convictions. The first reason is that the whole life of the people of Great Britain is based upon Christian tradition. We today—even those among us who are positively anti-Christian—are inheritors of this Christian tradition; it pervades every aspect of our life, from details of social good manners to basic points of the law. Consequently, the thoughts of any group of Christians on matters touching closely upon the law of the land and social morality have an intrinsic relevance. The second reason is that the authors are contributing, each from his knowledge and experience in his own field, their views as to the implications in medicine, society and the law of the suggestion that euthanasia should be legalised. Each of them from his own point of view has formed the same opinion on the subject of euthanasia. Their views are not based on preconceptions, but on careful thought. The thinking of Christians draws upon a great heritage of sound philosophy, but this is not to say that Christians are incapable of reasoning except on purely doctrinal Christian assumptions. The authors of this work have tried to approach the subject in what might simply be called a humanist manner, leaving aside from their reasoning such insight as they may gain from faith.

This humanist approach is very different from the approach of, for example, a professional theologian, founding his argument on the knowledge of God and man which we have by revelation. Yet however different the didactic method might be, there is no doubt that the final judgment would be the same : however the question is approached, once it is thought through carefully, it can be answered only in one way—that it would be disastrous to introduce into the law of the land even the germ of the idea that it could ever be right for a doctor or a nurse to kill a patient, no matter what statutory limitations and controls might be prescribed. It is true that the propaganda in favour of euthanasia is supported by not a few eminent persons, but the present authors believe that the view they present in this book is that of the majority of lawyers, doctors and nurses and will remain so because it is the view that best accords with all that we know of man and human society.

The authors offer this book in the hope that it may contribute to a better public understanding of what is at stake in the matter of euthanasia, before any rash measures are urged upon Parliament.

Chapter II

History and development of the euthanasia movement

I. Early Times and Primitive People

Among certain primitive people, the killing or abandonment of aged or helpless members was an accepted practice. The Hottentots, for example, were accustomed to carry their elderly parents out into the bush to die. Of the Lapps, P. Caraman writes: 'Less than a hundred years ago it is said that when old Lapp folk became too infirm to trek over the mountains with their families, they were left behind to die unattended in these tents. The corpse froze and was buried on the family's return. Some writers believe that the Lapps used another method of disembarrassing themselves of their old people : strapped to a sleigh alive, they were shot down the steep snow-covered precipice into the fjord. This is the end they expected and they submitted to it uncomplaining. It is thought also that when an old woman was near death she would be given a cold bath to hasten her dying.'[1] Similar practices have been related of some Eskimos, but again without very full corroboration. On the other hand, many primitive societies have been shown to have elaborate social codes which actually protected the senior member of the tribe. Instances of this are seen in hospitality customs, property rights, food taboos reserving certain choice dishes for the aged (ostensibly as harmful to the young), and other usages. Settled agricultural communities showed the highest level of solicitude for their elderly members, and this is well exemplified by the

[1] P. Caraman, *Norway*, Longmans, Green & Co. Ltd. (1969), page 155.

laws of the Hebrews in the Old Testament, forbidding the killing of the 'innocent and just', and in their general attitude of respect for the old. Even hunting people like the Iroquois Indians were capable of considerable reverence and kindliness towards their elderly even if helpless or mentally disordered. In fact, many primitive societies had a pattern of social insurance for the old which modern society would do well to view with respect.

In classical Greece there does not seem to have been any abandonment of elderly or helpless adults, though Plato was critical of one Herodicus for prolonging the life of sick elderly people. The Hippocratic Oath declared 'I will give no deadly drug to any, though it be asked of me, nor will I counsel such. . . .' In Sparta, although it was a military society, there was a considerable respect for the old, and there is no evidence, despite the acceptance of infant-exposure as a normal practice, that there was any policy of elimination of sick or helpless adults.

In ancient Rome, largely due to the influence of the Stoics, suicide was an accepted form of death (as it was at least until recently in Japan under the form of hara-kiri) as an escape from disgrace or from death at the hands of enemies or political opponents. And yet Cicero in a remarkable passage wrote: 'The God that rules within us forbids us to depart hence unbidden', and he had the courage to put his beliefs into practice for he declined to play 'the Roman fool' when pursued to death by the revenge of Antony. Seneca the Younger, on the other hand, expressed the then more current view when he stated: 'If one death is accompanied by torture and the other is simple and easy, why not snatch the latter? Just as I select my ship when I am about to go on a voyage, and my house when I propose to take a residence, so shall I choose my death when I am about to depart from life. Moreover, just as a long drawn-out life does not necessarily mean a better one, so a long drawn-out death necessarily means a worse one.' He too acted in conformity with his opinion, for when accused of conspiracy he accepted the choice of death by his own hand.

By contrast, infanticide has been widely practised. Primitive societies and earlier civilisations have often decreed that weakly or diseased infants should be put to death by active means or passively by exposure. In addition to this, girl babies in particular have often been eliminated for what might be termed social reasons. Warrior or hunting tribes, finding too large a female population an encumbrance, eliminated a proportion of girls. High caste Rajputs once did the same, for economic reasons, since it was at one and the same time dishonourable to a family to leave girls unmarried and extremely costly to marry them to men of their own caste. This was done despite the fact that the Vedas forbade such practices. In Sparta and other City States of classical Greece weak or deformed babies were exposed, the practice meeting with the approval of both Aristotle and Plato. Plato, in the *Republic,* went further and advocated eugenic breeding : '. . . the children of the worst father and mother, or others that are diseased, will be put away secretly and no one will know what has become of them'.

Jewish, Christian and Islamic teachings alike have always maintained that deliberate killing in cases of abnormality or incurable illness is wrong, and this practice has always been forbidden in Jewish, Christian and Islamic communities. There is, however, an interesting, albeit imaginary, exception to this rule at the time of the Renaissance. St Thomas More's Utopians allowed euthanasia provided that

(i) the patient's illness was incurable and caused anguish, and

(ii) the patient freely consented either to take his own life or be put to sleep after persuasion by the priests and the Council.

Many of the supporters of euthanasia have quoted this as evidence of More's true opinion, even expressing surprise in view of it that Catholics should be opposed to euthanasia. However, to do this is to miss the whole point of *Utopia* by supposing that More (whose own family sometimes could not tell whether he was joking or in earnest) was expressing his own view as a Catholic. What More was concerned to do in his delicate satire was to describe a non-Christian society and to show how in many ways it was to be preferred to the Renaissance societies of his own time. This is not to say that he approved of all the practices of the Utopians: on the contrary he wrote, 'I have only undertaken to give you an account of their constitution, but not to defend all their principles.'

Individuals have been recorded at various times as taking personal action in this respect, but this has never been morally approved. Thus, Ambroise Paré, surgeon to Francis I in Turin in 1537, mentions that finding several severely wounded and unconscious men: '. . . an old soldier asked me if there was any way to cure them. I said "No". Then he went up to them and cut their throats, gently and without ill will. I told him he was a villain; he answered he prayed God that when he should be in such a plight, he might find someone to do the same for him.' Similar instances can be recalled in more recent times, and there have been lenient judgments in 'mercy killing' cases, but there has not been any wider acceptance of the practice, nor any attempt to regularise it until the modern euthanasia movement.

II. 1870 to the Present Day

In 1873 L. A. Tollemache, in an eloquent and persuasive article,[2] made a strong plea for the legalisation of voluntary euthanasia. This was in support of a similar proposal made during the previous year by S. D. Williams. In a subsequent article, *The Spectator* stated:

> It appears to be quite evident, though we do not think it is expressly stated in Mr Tollemache's article, that much the strongest arguments to be alleged for putting an end to human sufferings apply to cases where you cannot be any possibility have the consent of the sufferer to that course.[3]

Thus rebutted, and in common with all advocates of euthanasia who have impressed public opinion, Tollemache at once issued an apologia. He went so far as to concede that in a case of extreme suffering where consent could not be obtained, the

[2] 'The New Cure of Incurables', *Fortnightly Review* 19 (1873) 218.
[3] 'Mr Tollemache and the Right to Die', *The Spectator* 46 (1873) 206.

dying person should be allowed to linger on and die a natural death.

Apart from some minor stirrings arising mainly from press reports of various 'mercy killings', very little of import took place until 1931. This was the year of birth of the euthanasia movement in Britain. The date was 16 October and the event the Presidential Address to the Society of Medical Officers of Health. The agent was Dr C. Killick Millard, at the time Medical Officer of Health for the City of Leicester.

Dr Millard startled his audience by devoting his complete address[4] to a plea for the legalisation of voluntary euthanasia, and the consideration of a draft Bill entitled 'The Voluntary Euthanasia (Legalisation) Bill'. He began by asserting that the majority of people who die do so in extreme pain. The ever-increasing mortality from cancer would have the effect of increasing the proportion of painful deaths. He reminded his listeners that common humanity demands that we put down a diseased or mutilated animal, and that if we neglect to do so we are guilty of cruelty. He quoted at length from the apparent apologia in More's *Utopia*.

Dr Millard then proceeded to a long comparative study of the morals of suicide and euthanasia. His information on the subject was based mainly on Westermark's work, *The Origin and Development of Moral Ideas*. He contrasted the situation in some countries, e.g. Japan and India, where suicide under certain circumstances was regarded with respect, with that in Christian countries. Dr Millard's argument appears to have been that whereas suicide (excluding the large group of persons whose minds are unbalanced) must always be wrong, euthanasia (under certain conditions) must always be right. His address also included the statement:

But there are cases where suicide is resorted to because a man believes, rightly or wrongly, that it will always be better for his loved ones if he is 'out of the way'. Such cases are to be deprecated because it is not for a man to decide for himself

[4] Printed in *Public Health*, November 1931.

about such an irrevocable step, and he may so easily be mistaken. Pity, however, rather than censure should be the predominant sentiment in such cases. Legalised voluntary euthanasia would come into quite a different category, as an act which was rational, courageous, and often highly altruistic.

Dr Millard then referred in detail to his draft Bill on the subject. This Bill is considered in Chapter III.

Following his dissertation on his legislative proposals Dr Millard, with disarming naivety, told his audience :

The procedure . . . may sound a little complicated, though in reality it is not much more so than the procedure which has to be gone through in the case of cremation.

It is perhaps easier in retrospect than it was for Dr Millard at the time to understand how these strenuous efforts were in a few years to be defeated by the very complexity of the proposals put forward.

While extensive publicity was accorded to Dr Millard's address by the national press, opinion was guarded and non-committal. *The Universe* alone appears to have raised its editorial voice firmly in protest.

On the other hand there was a minor surge of support in the form of letters to Dr Millard from many people, including eminent churchmen and members of the medical profession. This support led directly to Dr Millard's foundation in 1935 of the Euthanasia Society.[5] Many distinguished people were soon numbered among its members, under the presidency of the first Lord Moynihan, himself one of the foremost surgeons of his time. Its avowed objects were to :

Create a public opinion favourable to the view that an adult person suffering severely from a fatal illness for which no cure is known, should be entitled by law to the mercy of a painless

[5] The Voluntary Euthanasia Legalisation Society was founded in December 1935. In 1961 the Society's name was changed to the Euthanasia Society, and again in November 1969 to the Voluntary Euthanasia Society.

death if and when that is his expressed wish : and to promote this legislation.

The Society was so imbued with confidence that the Bill as originally elaborated by Dr Millard was ready for promotion in Parliament in the following year. Lord Moynihan having died a few months previously, the Second Reading in the House of Lords was moved by Lord Ponsonby of Shulbrede on 1 December 1936.

After an interesting and important debate (which is summarized on pages 38–44) the Bill was refused a second reading by 35 votes to 14.

The example set by the Euthanasia Society in Great Britain was followed in the United States when the Euthanasia Society of America was constituted in 1938 by the Rev Charles Potter. A Bill, following the British model, was introduced in the Nebraska Assembly in the same year, but was also lost. The same result attended an attempt to introduce a Bill in the New York Assembly. In Connecticut there is an apparently separate Voluntary Euthanasia Society. The Euthanasia Society of America had at first proposed to advocate the compulsory 'euthanasia' of monstrosities and imbeciles but, as a result of replies to a questionnaire addressed to physicians in the State of New York in 1941, it decided to limit itself to propaganda for voluntary euthanasia.

Following these defeats in Britain and the United States the fortunes of the euthanasia movement declined. Rumours of euthanasia in Nazi Germany and the revelations of the Nuremberg Trials did little to re-assure public opinion that the legalisation of voluntary euthanasia was not the 'thin edge of the wedge'.

However, in 1950 the House of Lords debated a motion in favour of voluntary euthanasia. As in the debate on the 1936 Bill, the House was clearly impressed by the weight of argument against legalised euthanasia adduced by those peers who were members of the medical profession. This debate is summarised on pages 44–49. The motion was purely one for debate, and was withdrawn without being voted upon, this being usual House of Lords procedure on such motions.

In the same year, 1950, the General Assembly of the World Medical Association approved a resolution recommending to all national associations that they 'condemn the practice of euthanasia under any circumstances'. Nevertheless, two years later a petition for the amendment of the Declaration on Human Rights to provide for incurable sufferers to have the right of voluntary euthanasia was presented to the United Nations by a number of British and American clergymen, doctors and scientists. It bore only 2513 signatures.

As in the thirties so in the fifties a personality appeared on the scene to provide the movement with fresh impetus. Professor Glanville Williams is a Fellow of Jesus College and Rouse Ball Professor of the Laws of England in the University of Cambridge. A former Professor of Public Law and Quain Professor of Jurisprudence in the University of London, he has been a member of the Standing Committee on Criminal Law Revision since 1959. His address to the Euthanasia Society on the occasion of the Annual General Meeting in 1955 could be said to have initiated a new phase. His keen legal mind analysed the cause of the failure of the 1936 Bill and the continuing opposition in 1950. Professor Glanville Williams realised that a Bill with too many safeguards would fail as would one with too few, and that a compromise solution must be found. He assumed from statements of Lord Dawson and Lord Horder that euthanasia was widely practised by the medical profession. He stressed that as the law now stands, cutting short the act of dying is permitted, but not anything done to anticipate death—which is a technical way of saying to precipitate death—though he could not see any 'logical or moral chasm' between the two, and he deprecated this laissez-faire attitude of the medical opponents of the proposed legislation.

Nevertheless there is, as Professor Glanville Williams somewhat ruefully admits, no country in the world whose law permits euthanasia. In France and Switzerland a doctor may provide, but may not administer, poison at the request of a patient suffering from a fatal illness. This distinction might seem to be artificial, but it is explicable on the ground that as suicide is not a crime in those countries, to be an accessory to it cannot be an offence either, but directly to kill another even from humane motives is still murder. According to Norwegian law, a judge may reduce the penalty for euthanasia below the prescribed minimum. In Russia suicide is not a crime, but to influence a dependent person to commit suicide is a crime punishable by imprisonment for five years, and to instigate a dependent person to commit suicide is also a criminal offence if that person is an adult or minor known to be incapable of understanding the nature or significance of his acts.

It is not possible, therefore, to examine any existing legislation for euthanasia; the only precedents are the Bill introduced into the House of Commons in 1936, that subsequently presented in the Nebraska Assembly, the draft prepared by the Euthanasia Society in 1968 following the impetus given to the movement by Professor Glanville Williams and based on previous drafts, and that presented in the House of Lords in 1969 by Lord Raglan.

Chapter III

Legislative proposals
Comments on Bills and draft Bills
1936-1969

In the last chapter we saw how a movement in favour of euthanasia had been built up from the 1870's to the present time, and noted that no country had ever legislated in favour of it so that it was not possible to study euthanasia in action. There are however the various Bills and draft Bills to study and these give us some indication of how a law permitting euthanasia might be phrased.

The 1936 Bill

First then, the 1936 Bill. This is the Bill originally drafted by Dr Millard and referred to on page 26; it was the first Bill on euthanasia to be brought before the United Kingdom Parliament.

In the 1936 Bill, before euthanasia could be effected, the patient had

(i)   to be over twenty-one years of age,
(ii) to be suffering from an incurable and fatal illness, and
(iii) to sign a form in the presence of two witnesses asking to be put to death.

This form, accompanied by two medical certificates, had then to be submitted to an official appointed by the Minister of Health, called the 'Euthanasia Referee', who had to interview the patient and ensure that he meant what he asked for. He had also the right to call and question the practitioners and various relatives. If he was satisfied he would issue a certificate. The application, the medical certificate, and the referee's certificate had then to come before a special court. This court in its turn had the right to call and question the referee, the practitioners or relatives. Objections to the proposal would be considered, then if the court was satisfied, it would issue two certificates, one to the applicant and another to the practitioner deputed to administer euthanasia. The death itself had to be administered in the presence of an official witness—a justice of the peace, barrister, solicitor, doctor, minister of religion, or registered nurse.

The Nebraska Bill of 1938

The Nebraska Bill of 1938 was somewhat similar. Euthanasia was defined as 'the termination of life by painless means for the purpose of ending physical suffering'. Again the patient had to be over twenty-one years of age and suffering 'severe physical pain caused by a disease for which no remedy, lasting relief or recovery is at the time known to medical science'. The disease, however, did not have to be fatal. Curiously there was added a provision that the desire to anticipate death by euthanasia in those conditions was not to be deemed to indicate mental impairment. As in the U.K. Bill, the procedure was complicated, involving the court, a committee, petitions and appeals.

The 1968 draft Bill

In considering the terms of a new draft Bill in 1968, Professor Glanville Williams realised that he had to meet the objection that elaborate safeguards would bring 'too much formality into the sick room and destroy the relationship between doctor and patient'.[1]

He therefore proposed a simple formula: he suggested that it should merely be provided that 'no medical practitioner should be guilty of an offence in respect of an act done intentionally to accelerate the death of a patient who is seriously ill, unless it is

---

[1] G. Williams, *The Sanctity of Life and the Criminal Law*, Faber and Faber (1968), page 298.

proved that the act was not done in good faith with the consent of the patient and for the purpose of saving him from severe pain in an illness believed to be of an incurable and fatal character'.[2]

The draft Bill published by the Euthanasia Society in 1968 was framed to avoid unpleasant 'death-bed formalities' by providing that anyone might make a declaration in advance stating that he or she wished in certain circumstances to be put painlessly to death.

Anyone who made a declaration in the form set out in the First Schedule to the 1968 draft Bill became what the draft Bill called a 'qualified patient' once two physicians—one of whom had to have consultant status—had certified in writing that the patient appeared to them to be suffering from what was termed an 'irremediable condition'. In the draft Bill the term 'irremediable condition' meant one of three states :

(a) physical illness thought in the patient's case to be incurable and terminal and

(b) grievous physical affliction occasioning the patient serious injury or disability, thought to be permanent and expected to cause him severe distress;

(c) physical brain damage or deterioration so that the patient's normal mental faculties were severely and irreparably impaired.

It was then provided that a physician might lawfully 'administer euthanasia' to a 'qualified patient'.

Once a declaration was made it was not to come into effect until one month had elapsed, but then, unless revoked, was to remain in force during the lifetime of the declarant. A declaration could be revoked at any time, either by its destruction or by a notice of cancellation on its face, and the destruction or notice of cancellation could be effected either by the declarant or by his order. The declaration was normally to be kept by the declarant's own doctor, but anyone who had the keeping of it and who learnt that the declarant was an in-patient in a hospital

[2] G. Williams, *op. cit.*, page 303.

had to forward the declaration to the physician in charge of the declarant at the hospital.

All physicians, nurses and other persons were to be under a duty to report to the physician in charge at the hospital a patient's wish for euthanasia and the physician in charge had to ensure that the patient was then enabled to make a declaration. Subject to that, however, no physician or nurse was to be required to take any steps for furthering the administration of euthanasia if he or she was opposed in principle to this practice.

Any individual might carry on his person a short form of memorandum which could be either a card or a token as set out in the Second and Third Schedules to the draft Bill, and any person carrying such a card or token was to be presumed in an emergency to have made a declaration without any omission.

It was to be an offence punishable on indictment by a sentence of life imprisonment wilfully to conceal, destroy, falsify or forge a declaration or memorandum under the Bill.

In order to remove doubt, it was stated in the draft Bill that anyone suffering from an illness thought to be incurable and terminal should be entitled to have such sedation as would keep him continuously unconscious.

The Bill Debated in the Lords, 1969

Further changes were made in the Bill, which was actually presented in the House of Lords by Lord Raglan, and debated on Second Reading on 25 March 1969. This Bill was some improvement on the previous draft. Certain defects were remedied —for example, euthanasia might only be administered to a person who had attained the age of majority—but the scheme proposed was substantially the same as that contained in the 1968 draft. This Bill is reproduced in full in the Appendix (pages 136ff.), but as there are certain points in the drafting of the Bill whose significance is not fully apparent from the Explanatory Memorandum it is pertinent here to examine the Bill very briefly clause by clause, and refer to certain of the more obvious difficulties.

Any person, apparently even if under the age of majority, might make a declaration substantially in the form set out in the Schedule to the Bill. Once made the declaration did not come into effect for thirty days. Thereafter it remained in force for three years (unless revoked) but if re-executed within twelve months preceding its expiry it was valid for the lifetime of the declarant, unless revoked. Revocation might be effected either by the destruction of the declaration or by a notice of cancellation on its face, and the destruction might be done or the notice written either by the declarant or at his order.

Clause 1(2)

Clause 2

Clause 3

A person was a 'qualified patient' if he was over the age of majority and if two physicians—i.e. registered medical practitioners—one of whom had consultant status, certified in writing that he appeared to them to be suffering from an irremediable condition. An irremediable condition was defined as meaning a serious physical illness or impairment reasonably thought in the patient's case to be incurable and expected to cause him severe distress or to make him incapable of rational existence.

Clause 1(2)

A declarant who became a qualified patient might have euthanasia administered to him by a physician or by a state registered or state enrolled nurse carrying out treatment prescribed by a physician. Euthanasia was defined as the painless inducement of death.

Clause 1(1)

Clause 4(2)

Before administering euthanasia to a mentally responsible patient the physician had to make sure to his reasonable satisfaction that the declaration and all steps proposed to be taken under it accorded with the patient's wishes.

Clause 1(2)

Clause 4(1)

There was a satisfactory and unambiguous conscience clause, and equally, protection was afforded to all who administered euthanasia to a qualified patient in accordance with what was believed to be the patient's declaration and wishes.

Clause 4(3)

Clause 5

33

As in the 1968 draft, it was to be an offence punishable on indictment by life imprisonment wilfully to conceal, destroy, falsify or forge a declaration under the Bill; and a witness putting his signature to a statement *Clause* known by him to be false was to be deemed to have *6* committed an offence under the Perjury Act, 1911.

There was also a clause similar to that in the 1968 draft whereby it was provided for the removal of doubt that a patient suffering from an irremediable condition reasonably thought to be terminal should be entitled to receive drugs in quantities sufficient to keep him free *Clause* from pain and also to render him continuously un- *8* conscious if there was no other way of relieving severe distress.

Clause A provision not in the 1968 draft Bill made an *7* insurance policy valid if effected twelve months before the administration of euthanasia.

Clause Power was also given to the Secretary of State for *9* Social Services to make regulations.

It may be doubted whether a declaration is the best method of dealing with the aims which the Euthanasia Society wish to achieve. What may be gaily signed at the age of twenty may appear much more menacing at the age of sixty. Old persons, having signed a declaration in the form specified by the Bill are, if they change their mind, likely to be extremely worried about its cancellation.

The declaration presumably would have to be made by a person of sound mind; but there is nothing in the Bill to say so. It was only provided in the form set out in the Schedule that the witnesses had to state that the declarant appeared to appreciate its significance. And as has already been said, there was nothing to indicate at what age the declaration could be made.

The provision for the revocation of the declaration appears to have been defective. A declarant might not have his declaration and might be uncertain where it was, especially if he were then in the throes of a serious illness. In that event it would have been difficult for him to effect revocation in accordance with Clause 3, and this could well have been a cause of much anxiety. No provision was made for revocation by a fresh declaration.

The unsatisfactory nature of the declaration procedure was summed up, when the Bill was debated in the Lords, by the Bishop of Durham in these words : 'My view is that the un-doubted need for a declaration brings with it so many difficulties that the Bill turns out to be not for the benefit of humanity but to its detriment.'[3]

The definition of 'irremediable condition' was so wide that it could have applied to a person who has suffered a severe coronary thrombosis or stroke, the loss of one or more limbs, or a serious accident involving permanent physical or psychological consequences. It will be noted that the illness or impairment did not have to be fatal. It is not clear what was meant by the words 'incapable of rational existence' in the definition. No mention was made in the Bill about mental illness.

Clause 4 made provision for the ascertainment of the patient's wishes if he was mentally responsible. Nothing was said about what was to happen if the patient was not responsible mentally.

While the protection and safeguards set out in Clause 4 and 5 might be considered generally satisfactory, no provision was made to prohibit discrimination against doctors or nurses who are conscientiously opposed to euthanasia. A precedent might be found in Section 29 of the Education Act, 1944, which forbids, except in aided and special agreement schools, any refusal to appoint or promote a teacher either because he does or does not give religious instruction or attend religious worship. It may per-haps be argued, however, cynically but realistically that no statutory provision will prevent discrimination of this sort : persons who for the sake of conscience will not perform actions which are expected (such, for example, as abortions) are not appointed or promoted ostensibly for quite different reasons.

It is, moreover, somewhat bizarre to see in Clause 5(2) an exemption proposed to be granted to 'physicians and nurses who have taken part in the administration of euthanasia' from any

[3] Hansard, H. of L., 25 March 1969, vol 300, col 1181.

professional oath or affirmation. What presumably was intended was relief from that part of the Hippocratic Oath which states 'I will give no deadly drug to any, though it should be asked of me, nor will I counsel such'. It was not thought necessary in the Abortion Act to provide relief from the next words of the Oath 'and especially I will not aid a woman to procure abortion'. It would be unfortunate if a precedent were established of affording statutory protection for the breach of oaths freely and solemnly sworn.

The maximum penalty proposed in both the 1968 draft and in Lord Raglan's Bill for concealing, destroying, falsifying or forging a declaration seems to be extremely excessive, except in the case of relatives who forge a declaration or memorandum for the purposes of having a rich or unwanted relative or spouse put to death. It seems incongruous that a Bill which serves to exempt doctors and nurses from the crime of murder, now punishable by life imprisonment, should contain a clause making the tampering with a declaration a crime punishable with the same maximum penalty.

Few would object to a person being kept under deep sedation if he is suffering from an incurable and fatal illness. This is euthanasia in its literal meaning of a painless death and not in its morbid meaning of a painless killing. Nevertheless, the provision in Clause 8 of the Bill is open to strong objection as was pointed out by several speakers in the debate in the House of Lords. This is further discussed in Chapter V.

Unlike the Abortion Act, the Bill somewhat surprisingly did not contain any provisions about where euthanasia could be performed. If this Bill had become law, the Secretary of State for Social Services might have made regulations on this subject under Clause 9(1). It might be thought that there was a hint of this in the words of that clause about the Secretary of State having to make regulations 'for appointing (with their consent) hospital physicians having responsibility in relation to patients who have made or wish to make a declaration'. These words are obscure, but it seems possible that they meant rather to echo the provisions in the draft Bill of 1968 about the declaration of an in-patient in a hospital having to be forwarded to the physician in charge of the declarant in that hospital and for that physician, on hearing of his patient's wish for euthanasia, to ensure that he was enabled to make a declaration.

Chapter IV

Parliament debates euthanasia 1936-1970

There have been four important debates on euthanasia in the United Kingdom Parliament. These are of particular interest as the various arguments adduced by the speakers reflect closely the arguments for and against euthanasia put forward at public meetings, and expressed in pamphlets, books, and letters to the newspapers in the 1930's, in the 1950's and in recent years. Of those four debates, three have been in the House of Lords and one in the House of Commons. The following summaries of these debates are condensed from the verbatim reports in Hansard.

A Bill Rejected

The first debate took place in the House of Lords on 1 December 1936,[1] when the Second Reading of the 'Voluntary Euthanasia (Legalisation) Bill' was moved by Lord Ponsonby of Shulbrede. This was to have been done by Lord Moynihan, but he had died the previous August. This Bill was introduced into Parliament in the House of Lords, that is to say it had not been debated in the House of Commons.

LORD PONSONBY, moving the Second Reading, said that there were three opinions about the Bill: some approved in principle and thought the safeguards satisfactory; some approved in principle, but were doubtful about the adequacy of the safeguards; others disapproved in principle.

He quoted many eminent clerics and medical men among the

[1] Hansard, H. of L., vol 103, cols 465-506.

supporters of the principle. He admitted that the medical profession was not in full agreement with the Bill, but then it was not a purely medical matter. It was also ethical, social and legal.

He summarised the principle of the Bill in Lord Moynihan's words: 'Briefly our desire is to obtain legal recognition for the principle that in cases of advanced and inevitably fatal disease, attended by agony which reaches, or oversteps, the boundaries of human endurance, the sufferers after legal enquiry and after due observance of all safeguards, shall have the right to demand and be entitled to receive release.'

Suicide was sometimes excusable. John Donne had said, 'It is a wayward and unnoble stubborness in argument to say, still I must not kill myself but I may let myself die.' The philosopher Hume also had a passage, which he quoted, that in certain circumstances suicide was laudable. Father Damien, the leper missionary, 'knew he was going to kill himself', as did Captain Oates in the Antarctic. The distinction between noble self-sacrifice and suicide to avoid pain was untenable; consideration for others was often uppermost in the minds of those seeking death. At present some doctors overcame their fear of the law and administered fatal doses. Narcotics in big doses shortened life anyway.

He considered that the support from clergy showed that euthanasia was not contrary to Christian teaching. He was surprised that Catholics should oppose it in view of the words of St Thomas More in *Utopia*: '. . . if the disease be not only incurable, but also full of continual pain, and anguish; then the priests and the magistrates exhort the man, seeing he is not able to do any duty of life, and by over-living his own death is noisome and irksome to others, and grievous to himself; that he will determine with himself no longer to cherish that pestilent and painful disease. And seeing that his life is to him but a torment, that he will not be unwilling to die, but rather take a good hope to him, and either dispatch himself out of that painful life as out of a prison, or a rack of torment, or else suffer himself to be rid out of it by other. And in so doing they tell him he shall do wisely, seeing that by his death he shall lose no commodity, but end his pain.' There was not a shred of evidence, he said, to show that

that was not what More considered to be the ideal. Courage in the face of pain was no doubt a virtue, but one had to consider the other feelings of a patient in agony when he saw his friends around him and knew he was a burden to them.

Legal opinions were beginning to incline to leniency. In 1927 a man drowned his sick daughter: Mr Justice Branson said that if the child had been an animal the man would have been punished for not destroying it. In another case Mr Justice Goddard had hinted at a desirable change in the law. The leniency in these cases showed that the law was being stretched to accord with public opinion. 'We have restricted our proposals in this Bill purposely, whatever our views may be about Mongolians (*sic*), congenital idiots and senile dementia, . . .' 'In cases under this Bill initiative comes from the patient . . . We are not opening any door, we are merely unlocking it. We are drawing the bolts by which prejudice and tradition have kept it closed.'

He then went through the Bill in detail and dealt with various minor points, like the effect on life assurance. He also said that he would be ready to accept constructive amendments.

LORD DENMAN to allay fears emphasised the limited scope of the Bill. Horses and dogs, he said, were put down painlessly—only human beings had to suffer to the end. If it was true that euthanasia was already practised by certain doctors, it was intolerable for such doctors to have to take the risk of acting illegally. The Bill would end the mental stress of those who were forced to sit idly by, unable to alleviate or end the sufferings of those they loved.

VISCOUNT FITZALAN OF DERWENT moved that the Bill be read this day six months. (This is the standard form in which the rejection of a Second Reading is formally moved in the House of Lords.)

Those who opposed euthanasia on account of their religious tenets were entitled to oppose the Bill on its merits, as detrimental to the welfare of the country. Notwithstanding the voluntary nature of the Bill, the relatives would have great responsibility thrust upon them. He was sorry for the doctors who had to 'perpetrate the act' and most sorry for the mental agony of the patient while the formalities were being prepared for his demise. Admittedly some medical opinion was in favour, but much was also against the Bill. A doctor in the civil service had recently said that euthanasia, even voluntary, was pregnant with criminal possibilities.

It was not only Catholics who opposed the Bill. It was against the law of nature, which branded it as evil and a cowardly act. Orthodox Jews and Mohammedans were against it. Those who denied that there was a God had to judge on sentiment, and uncontrolled sentiment led to abandonment of principle. The Bill sought to arrogate to man the right of God to decide when life should end; this was an impertinence.

LORD DAWSON OF PENN said that from the speeches people might get the impression that agonising pain was more common than in fact it was. Even in fatal cancer, pain was an outstanding feature in less than half the cases. There was a steady growth in doctors' power to assuage pain. Modern patients did not lack courage, but nowadays there seemed to be less value placed upon life which had become useless. Fifty years ago the medical profession concentrated on prolonging life to the limit in any circumstances, but now doctors and others thought it best to ease the passing of a patient even if it meant shortening life. Doctors did not lay down edicts for these matters; there had been a general and silent change in attitude. No change of statute law was needed for this evolution of practice. As comparable examples he quoted contraception, abortion and suicide; attitudes had changed and practices with them, without a change of statute.

The procedure of the Bill 'would turn the sick room into a bureau'. It was unpleasantly like the procedure for certifying the insane. It might even reverse the trend towards euthanasia. He confessed surprise at Lord Fitzalan's remarks and quoted a Catholic book as saying that it was lawful to use drugs to alleviate pain even though it was foreseen that these would shorten life, provided that the alleviation of pain, and not the shortening of life, was the primary purpose of the drug. He added 'that is what we feel would be the right attitude of mind. We have not in mind to set to work to kill anybody at all.'

THE ARCHBISHOP OF CANTERBURY (Dr Lang) said there were cases where life could be laid down without blame for the sake of others, but it was quite different to give statutory authority to a man in his own interest and for his own sake to end his life. If that were done, many would justify their own suicide by comparing circumstances. There would be unforeseen effects upon the public conscience of giving legal encouragement to the principle that in certain circumstances a man might end his own life.

Was a man in great pain capable of making a sound moral judgement? And would not the procedure be an intolerable strain? There could be illegitimate pressure on the sick man. He was not usually impressed by an argument from 'the thin end of the wedge' but in this case the promoters definitely contemplated its extension. 'If once the door is unlocked it will soon be opened wide.' He did not think suffering had to be borne as divine will; drugs were perfectly proper; but if they shortened life the propriety of their use was a matter for the doctors. It was a perversion of language to equate euthanasia with such use of drugs.

LORD HORDER said that doctors were sympathetic to efforts towards biological control, as being helpful to their work. But this Bill introduced a new principle and was outside the doctors' reference. 'The good doctor is aware of the distinction between prolonging life and prolonging the act of dying. The former comes within his reference, the latter does not.'

The Bill would cause an unwelcome re-orientation of the doctor's functions. The fact that euthanasia was to be administered by someone other than the customary physician was an illustration of the change. The introduction of 'strangers from Whitehall' was not in the patient's interest. How was the doctor to answer the question 'You will stand by me won't you, doctor?' The intricate procedure for application appalled him. He drew attention to the extreme difficulty of the duty of the referee; he had to certify the disease incurable. This could only be done on experience which was highly fallible. The criteria of incurability and fatality would become with time more and not less difficult to establish.

The Bill did not distinguish between physical and mental pain, the latter calling for psychological help rather than chemical anodynes. Soundness of mind was very difficult to prove, since the patient's mind was uncertain or variable. 'Will not some persons . . . misinterpret the raised eyebrows of some of their friends and consider that they ought to avail themselves of this legalised permit to ring down the curtain?' It was important to distinguish between the agony of the patient and that of his friends. To live was his inalienable right.

THE MARQUESS OF CREWE agreed that Lord Ponsonby appeared to be thinking not only of the physical pain but of the moral and mental anguish of the patient, and there was nothing about that in the Bill. The position would be very much complicated if that were to be taken into account together with such matters as the burden of the patient to a poor family.

He asked how soon death had to be anticipated for the illness to be described as fatal. Could euthanasia be applied for if death were to be expected a few years hence? There were sometimes unexpected cures and many had outlived by years their doctors' forecasts.

THE BISHOP OF NORWICH (The Rt. Rev. Bertram Pollock) urged that the elaborate nature of the safeguards themselves showed that there was some doubt in the minds of the promoters. He was in favour of letting the thought of the medical profession grow on the subject. It was wrong to argue from a comparison with animals; there was something higher in man which differentiated him wholly from other animals. It was not quite a religious question nor quite an ethical one. We were being asked to act in a sphere where we knew nothing. We could see the suffering of the patient, but when we came to the issues of life and death—that was different. We did not know, and it would be wrong to legislate as if we did. No one looked upon suffering with indifference, but the way to deal with the problem was on the lines suggested by Lord Dawson.

THE EARL OF LISTOWEL spoke as the Vice-President of the Society for the Legalisation of Voluntary Euthanasia. He noted that both the Archbishop and Lord Dawson of Penn had accepted that suicide was justifiable in certain circumstances and that Lord Horder had said a doctor could sometimes take the initiative. The present law put too great a burden on the doctor; he had to perform a criminal act to satisfy his moral conscience.

The opponents of the Bill were condemning people to days and perhaps months of acute agony. He wished to convince everyone of all religious persuasions that euthanasia was in accordance with what they believed. The cardinal point was the exercise of charity. The Bill sought to extend that and was therefore in keeping with the main body of Christian tradition. If the arguments were examined on their merits, the increased exercise of the spirit of compassion would be seen to outweigh all other arguments.

THE EARL OF CRAWFORD repudiated the charge of inhumanity in the opponents of the Bill—the charge was a travesty of the speeches against the Bill. The Bill would cause more suffering than it relieved. It would bring strife and lasting grief into families. He expressed his profound distress at the possibility of unconscious pressure on a patient, and disgust at the prospect of intrigues inherent in the complicated procedures. He deplored the dangers which must arise from an Act of Parliament with all the complications, clumsiness and tactlessness of an ill-considered measure.

VISCOUNT GAGE (for the Government) said that the Government did not desire to be dogmatic but if the House gave the Bill a Second Reading it would seek certain amendments. The Government did not wish to impose upon a section of the medical profession an obligation to do something which they considered wrong.

LORD PONSONBY OF SHULBREDE (clearly anticipating that the majority of the House was against him) said that the time would come when Parliament would have to regulate the matter.

The House divided: those in favour of the Bill 14; those against 35.

A Motion Not Well Received

The next debate in the House of Lords was on 28 November 1950.[2] This was not a debate on a Bill, but on a Motion in the

[2] Hansard, H. of L., vol. 169, cols 552-598.

name of Lord Chorley 'To call attention to the need for legalising voluntary euthanasia, and to move for papers'. This type of 'Motion for Papers' is the form in which a general debate on any subject is raised in the House of Lords. Although such a Motion can be, and very occasionally is, put to the vote, the usual procedure is for the peer who moved the Motion to rise at the end of the debate and ask leave to withdraw it. That was done on this occasion.

LORD CHORLEY referred to the 1936 Bill and to the change of opinion in favour of 'mercy killing', subject of course to safeguards. The object of the Motion was to enable legislation to be introduced 'to provide a man who is suffering from an illness involving severe pain, the illness being incurable and of a fatal character, with a merciful release from his suffering'.

He acknowledged the necessity for stringent safeguards, and reiterated the conditions in the 1936 Bill. He quoted the passage from *Utopia* describing the practice of euthanasia which Lord Ponsonby had quoted in 1936, and praised the compassion shown in the words. He then briefly described the Voluntary Euthanasia Legalisation Society of which he was a Vice-President.

Pain-killing drugs, he insisted, were quite inadequate. He had a childhood recollection of a friend of the family dying of cancer —this experience had converted him to voluntary euthanasia. There was not only the patient to be considered but those of his family looking after him whose lives could be ruined by the need to care for him.

Animals in suffering were put down—why not humans? He quoted judges as being sometimes in favour, including Lord Goddard (at that time Lord Chief Justice) and went on to list considerable numbers of eminent men who favoured euthanasia.

In the Debate on the Second Reading of the Bill in 1936, he continued, Lord Dawson of Penn had spoken in favour of euthanasia, although he had voted against the Bill. He implied that Lord Dawson had proposed that doctors should be able to put patients away at their own discretion, but at this he was interrupted by Lord Haden-Guest who was sure Lord Dawson had meant nothing of the sort.

Continuing, Lord Chorley said that some doctors practised euthanasia anyway; others had 'religious scruples'. 'Surely it is wrong that the wretched patient's chance of escape from his sufferings should have to depend on . . . who is his doctor.'

He considered the contrary arguments. First, that the safeguards were inadequate: he could deal with that argument if specific inadequacies were brought to his notice. Secondly, that the Bill did not go far enough—i.e. could not be applied to children. Legislation on the matter would have to proceed step by step, starting with those who could give consent.

But the most formidable argument, he said, came from the churches, based on religious conscience. To the principle that the Lord alone should take away what he had given there were exceptions, as capital punishment was an exception to the general law against killing. The personality was more important than life —life which we shared with the animals. Christianity emphasised the sacredness of personality.

While pain might sometimes strengthen the character, prolonged pain merely destroyed it. A man should be entitled to save his personality by freeing himself from his body. In any case, those who objected to euthanasia need not use the privileges granted to them under the Bill, but such people were not entitled to refuse relief to others.

LORD DENMAN supported the motion briefly, referring particularly to cancer.

THE ARCHBISHOP OF YORK (Dr Garbett) said 'For reasons both theological and social I find myself in opposition' to the motion. He granted that sometimes 'alleviation of pain is of greater importance than the prolonging of dying'. Once a licence to kill was granted, where would it stop? The feeble-minded and cripples would be included—like Nazi Germany's 'useless mouths'. Legislation on these lines would gradually weaken the value of human life. The dying would fear those about them and be embarrassed at the worry they caused to others: there could be no sufficient safeguard against that.

LORD HORDER said 'Putting an end to human life surely involves a new principle in biological control'. The doctor's duty was to cure, or, failing that, to prolong life while relieving pain. He agreed with the distinction implied by the Archbishop between prolonging life and prolonging the act of dying. 'Any sanction which would lead to a different orientation of the doctor's function . . . would not be in the public interest.'

His own experience indicated that the request for termination of life came mostly from those not in great pain, but in a state of 'misère'.

The criteria suggested for voluntary euthanasia he considered impractical. 'Incurable' and 'pain' were relative terms. A disease incurable today could be cured tomorrow, and different patients had different thresholds of pain. The morale of the patient was all important. 'The attitude of most patients is that of the soldier who wishes to face the enemy.'

He deemed illness and pain to have spiritual significance and value. He was suspicious of 'new ethics'.

The criterion of 'sound mind' was also relative. Many patients' minds were fitful and variable, so that an applicant for euthanasia in the morning could want to live in the afternoon. The agony of the others about the sick bed should not be taken into consideration.

THE EARL OF IDDESLEIGH corrected Lord Chorley's misunderstanding of *Utopia*. He pointed out that Lord Chorley's arguments would appeal to those who minimised the difference between animal and human life. Pain had a natural and supernatural value. The main objection to euthanasia rested on the sanctity of human life. It was wrong to create a class licensed to bring death—and foolish to give that function to doctors, the bringers of life and health.

There would be a temptation for others to make up the patient's mind for him, and the patient would fear that.

VISCOUNT ESHER, supporting the motion, described euthanasia as 'an evolutionary extension of liberty', comparable to divorce and birth control. The argument that it was open to abuse was urged against all forms of freedom, and was an argument in fact only in favour of safeguards. The argument that the doctors were against it he dismissed by saying that doctors had been against Florence Nightingale and against the National Health Service.

If human beings were above the animals, they should be better treated—i.e. they should be put out of their misery more readily. LORD AMULREE supported the Archbishop and Lord Horder. The concept of doctor as executioner would not improve doctor/patient relations. The existence of suffering was a challenge to research. Where, he asked, would it end—this 'step by step'?

LORD UVEDALE OF NORTH END said that euthanasia was a confession of failure. From experience of many diseases he deduced that only in very few cases could euthanasia be contemplated—and such cases would grow fewer. Even in such cases there was the danger of incorrect diagnosis, which he illustrated by examples. 'The problem should be approached with great caution, remembering with all humility that euthanasia is an admission of failure and a counsel of despair.'

LORD HADEN-GUEST said that advocates had not brought forward any improved arguments as compared with 1936. There was no evidence as to need : how many cases were there? Great advances were taking place in methods of treatment and in medicinal substances. On what evidence of doctors was the demand for euthanasia based? He knew of none. Once the principle was introduced, why should we not go the whole 'Hitler hog'? He concluded : 'As a doctor I . . . feel . . . a sense of outrage that this proposal has been brought before us.'

LORD WEBB JOHNSON observed that the medical members of the House were unanimous in rejecting the idea and he cited recent medical discoveries which had done much to relieve the pain of previously 'incurable' diseases.

THE EARL OF HUNTINGDON supported the motion, repeating the argument from the comparison with animals, and emphasising the voluntary nature of the proposed euthanasia. Interrupted by Lord Haden-Guest who asked him why the doctors should do the killing, Lord Huntingdon replied that he respected the reluctance of the medical profession to take on a new responsibility, but 'we have to consider the patient'.

The advocates of euthanasia were not asking religious people to adopt it—only to tolerate it when practised by those who did not share their views.

He reminded the House that if the safeguards were inadequate they could always be reviewed.

He did not accept the argument from the thin end of the wedge. The Hitler-style dictator would go his own way without bothering about the laws on euthanasia.

He did not consider the legalisation of euthanasia would undermine the confidence of the patient in his doctor. The doctor was not the arbiter. A patient would be able to rely on his doctor not merely to relieve pain but to take one further step if necessary. He therefore considered the added mental anxiety feared by many to be a negligible factor.

VISCOUNT ST DAVIDS spoke of the absolute value of human life. He agreed with Lord Iddesleigh's remarks. The claims of the advocates of euthanasia were much exaggerated.

THE LORD CHANCELLOR (Viscount Jowett) told the House that the Government were against the proposal. He was appalled at the bureaucratic procedure envisaged to allow one men legally to kill another. Euthanasia would have serious repercussions on the criminal law. The criteria were all relative and could not be proved in court. 'There can be no adequate safeguards where one human being is allowed to start killing another.'

'A Bill to legalise euthanasia would allow murder in certain circumstances; and the confines within which it is allowed can never be so clearly defined that we may not have people stepping outside them.' The only safe procedure was to allow the doctors to alleviate pain and suffering in the light of the recognised principles affecting both the quality and quantity of life.

Another Bill Rejected

The third debate in the House of Lords was the one on Lord Raglan's Bill on 25 March 1969.[3] Like the 1936 debate, this was the Second Reading debate of a Bill which was being

[3] Hansard, H. of L., vol 300, cols 1143-1254. Text of the Bill given in the Appendix, pages 136 ff.

introduced into Parliament in the House of Lords, and so had not been discussed by the House of Commons.

LORD RAGLAN moved the Second Reading. He thought public opinion was favourable to a change in the law and that the time was ripe to introduce a new Bill, incorporating changes (as against the 1936 Bill) in the formalities and safeguards.

Lord Longford's remarks on the Abortion Bill that it would be euthanasia next had been a safe prophecy, and the Bill was in line with recent measures such as the Suicide Act and others which betokened a change of attitude towards the freedom of the individual. There was less inclination to demand that the State should legislate in areas of private conscience and behaviour : on the contrary there was demand for the repeal of laws thought to be unwarrantably restrictive of private choice. The chief reason why euthanasia was not yet legal was that the patients who were its beneficiaries were not in a position to campaign for it.

Resuscitatory techniques increased the fear of a vegetative life among those maimed in body and mind, with personalities disintegrated, and though there were moral, ethical, religious, medical and practical objections to the Bill, he had been encouraged by overwhelming public support in its favour expressed in letters he had received. To kill onself was no longer a crime : this freedom should be extended to all those who wanted to terminate their lives. He paid tribute to Dr Saunders' work at St Christopher's Hospice,[4] but only a few could go to places like that. While it was good to strive to extend that type of work, his Bill would go hand in hand with that. It would be wrong to deny the Bill to those who needed it, upon moral grounds. Having lived to the full, people should be allowed to die at will.

Pain used to be regarded by many as good in itself, as a preparation for the 'great beyond'. Few thought like this now.

Many people distinguished between shortening and terminating

4 An undenominational religious foundation for the care of patients with terminal and advanced cancer and other long-term illnesses causing chronic pain or distress. It is outside the National Health Service but has contractual arrangements with the South-East Hospital Board and certain teaching hospitals, so that for the majority of patients its care is free. It is carrying out research into the control of pain and distress and the problems of bereaved families, and it has an intensive teaching programme.

life, 'but the principle has become established that it is better in terminal cases that a human being die than that he be allowed to suffer great pain'.

The BMA opposed the Bill: their objections amounted to 'leave it to us'. He quoted Dr Donald Gould on the withdrawal of antibiotics to help a sufferer 'over the edge'. A national opinion poll had established that 76.2% of doctors agreed that some doctors do help their patients 'over the last hurdle'.

The training of doctors in terminal care could be improved, but no improvement here would render the Bill unnecessary, for under the Bill patients could help the doctor in his difficulty of balancing between the duties of preserving life and alleviating suffering. The same national opinion poll which he had quoted showed 36.6% of doctors would be willing to administer euthanasia. Most doctors were already prepared to give drugs to relieve pain even if it shortened life. The doctors' dilemma was at its most acute when there was not pain but acute mental suffering. 'It is in conditions of this kind that a person may feel that he is no longer a person but just existing, perhaps a travesty of himself. Good doctors are aware of this feeling in a patient, but as the law stands there is nothing they can do.' The existence of a declaration would give the doctor ethical guidance as to his patient's wishes.

Lord Raglan then described in detail the provisions of the Bill. Finally, Lord Raglan turned to two objections. The first was that the doctor/patient relationship would be destroyed. He asserted that it would be improved, as patients would know that the doctor would help them to die. The second was that the Bill would cheapen life. To this he replied that increasingly the medical profession and others were concerned with the quality rather than the quantity of life.

THE EARL OF CORK AND ORRERY expressed some sympathy with the aims of the Bill, but he said 'I oppose the Bill because I believe it to be a bad Bill, inadequately thought out, ill-drafted and riddled with loopholes and ambiguities of the most dangerous kind; and above all because it fails in what it chiefly ought to do . . . it provides no reliable safeguards for the patient. . . . A few it even exposes to the risk of manslaughter and conceivably in extreme cases of murder.' The 'painless inducement of death' was not a good definition and set the tone of the draftsmanship. He read on with a suspicious eye.

The only safeguards in the Bill were the penalties for forging etc. a declaration, and the safeguards for the doctors and nurses. Presumably unintentionally, paragraph A of the declaration was an indemnification of manslaughter; the witnesses to it had to make six statements, of which five would be useless in any case that might be brought against them for perjury. Those five were (1) that the declarant 'appeared to appreciate' the significance of the declaration, (2) that the witnesses did not know of any pressure being brought on the patient, (3) that they believed it to be made by his own wish, (4) that so far as they were aware they were entitled to attest the declaration, and (5) that so far as they were aware they did not stand to benefit by the death of the declarant.

Lord Cork went on to describe the procedure as 'suicide by proxy'. Just one of the dangers was that the declaration could be used in circumstances not envisaged by the declarant, who might have signed it very many years previously. The Secretary of State could make regulations on anything he thought fit—which seemed to mean that practically anything after Clause 1(1) was redundant. How could we know what was the extent of the agony of another? But what would be the pressures brought upon a doctor by 'loving relations'! He concluded the Bill was incapable of amendment in Committee because it would emerge a virtually new Bill—'and a botched-up one at that'—and because a bill was not the best way of introducing a matter which needed wide and deep discussion. After all with advances in medical science the subject might not be suitable for legislation.

'We ought also to be sure that we have got the logic of the matter right, for if we have not, we may be setting in motion a logical train, the implications of which we shall find horrifying.' 'Who knows where we might be asked to go from there along the path that was followed in Nazi Germany?'
Lord Newton (Opposition Front Bench) said the main purpose

of the Bill was to allow one person to kill another in certain circumstances. This should never be lawful. Further, some of the details were immoral in themselves. The Bill ignored the fallibility of medical judgement, and the ever-increasing medical skill. A young man might sign a declaration and not be able to revoke it even though he wished to do so.

If suicide at one remove were to be made legal it ought, logically, to be made legal for all the circumstances in which men sought to kill themselves. Given the limitation in candidates, the Bill was unnecessary because of the existing practice of doctors referred to in Clause 8—and even these procedures were better not on the Statute Book. If the Bill was to be proceeded with it would have to be re-drafted from top to bottom. He asked what was a 'mentally responsible patient'—there was no statutory definition of mental responsibility. A patient's spouse or child could be imprisoned for life for concealing a document to avoid euthanasia being administered. He asked 'How barbarous can zealots become?' He pitied the Secretary of State who would have the heavy duty thrust on him under the Bill of regulating lawful homicide.

LORD AMULREE reminded the House that the use of drugs to relieve pain was nowadays much less distressing than in the days of opium and morphia. He quoted pre-war experience in a London home for the dying, emphasising the first-class care that made it a happy place. The training of doctors in ethical matters was of great importance. He praised the work of the London Medical Group in this connection. What was the demand for euthanasia? It did not come from the patients : occasionally it came from relatives, but that was a different matter. He remembered only one old lady asking to die, and she would not have been qualified under the Bill. Nevertheless, doctors had to avoid prolonging dying. If the old were a burden, the solution was to make proper provision for them. He quoted the French aphorism of the doctor's duty : 'Guérir quelquefois, soulager souvent, consoler toujours.'

LADY SEROTA (for the Government) said the Government were neutral on the Bill, but the administrative provisions were unacceptable. The doctors authorised by the Secretary of State would have the appalling duty of satisfying themselves of the validity of the declaration and on many other matters; moreover, as only hospital doctors—apparently—could be appointed, the patient's own doctor would not be able to administer euthanasia in the patient's home. It was not clear at what stage of a patient's illness he would become qualified; a patient might be suffering from an incurable illness but capable for a time of leading a reasonably satisfying life. She went on to quote Lord Horder in the 1950 Debate that 'it is a fact that the disease which is incurable today is cured next year'. These matters were important and very difficult. She also referred to fallibility of prediction. There was no valid check on the mental capacity of the patient at the time of signing the declaration, and no way of ascertaining in the case of a patient not mentally responsible what his wishes might have been had he been able fully to express them.

What help was it to a dead man if a declaration was afterwards found to have been forged? Or what protection had a patient who had asked for his declaration to be revoked if no action had been taken on that request?

Clause 8, she said, trespassed into the field of clinical judgement and its being in the Bill might be more damaging than helpful. She said her list of criticisms was not exhaustive, but sufficient to show the practical impossibilities of the Bill.

LORD BROCK's first reaction to the Bill was one of extreme distaste and dismay. Compassion could be a worthy motive, but it had to be controlled by reason. In the declaration even compassion was lost: signing a declaration was like joining a club; the idea was breathtaking in its naivety. His compassion for the sufferers did not lead him to support their killing by doctors. Doctors should have nothing to do with it. The patient's interests were paramount and his trust in his doctor would go if he felt that the doctor might kill him—that went for the nurse too. The argument that only the declarants would be affected was shallow and unacceptable.

If the state decided to kill off the aged, let it—but let it not ask the doctors to do so. He quoted from resolutions of the

Council of the British Medical Association, and from a report of its Central Ethical Committee, condemning euthanasia. No patient could be a proper judge of the desirability or inevitability of death. Patients and doctors could be mistaken.

He also described as breath-takingly naive the provision that physicians and nurses administering euthanasia should not be deemed to be in breach of any professional oath. Few medical people took a formal oath, but all had certain standards and principles which they considered binding upon them : this could not be evaded by Act of Parliament.

He thought Clause 8 unnecessary, and hoped the Bill would not be given a second reading.

THE BISHOP OF DURHAM (Rt. Rev. Ian Ramsey) said that Christians shared with others a respect for human life, and were guided by the example of Christ in healing and relieving distress. No man lived—or died—to himself, but in a social dimension.

He considered four possible contexts in which euthanasia might be used. In the context of pain, the arguments for euthanasia had been weakened by the progress of pharmacology. In the context of the maintenance of life by extraordinary means, something like euthanasia could be justified. In the context of severe mental distress, euthanasia would be at best problematical, not least because of our comparative ignorance of the matter. In the context of alleged social desirability, euthanasia was particularly hazardous. The Bill tried to cover too much. Even if euthanasia was justified, did the declaration help? 'My view is that the undoubted need for a declaration brings with it so many difficulties that the Bill turns out to be not for the benefit of humanity but to its detriment.'

The procedures under the Bill would increase fear and diminish confidence. In cases of the withdrawal of extraordinary means the doctors must be left to decide. This emphasised the necessity of ethical training of doctors. A declaration would expose doctors to pressures from relations and to agonising after-thoughts. The effect of the administration of euthanasia on other patients in a ward had to be considered. There was also the matter of the custody of declarations. He visualised hospitals and doctors getting the reputation of welcoming those who had made declarations, or of taking a wide view of 'severe distress', or even taking people's word for it that a declaration had been made. He pitied the poor nurse who had to administer euthanasia, for the difficulties, uncertainties and anxieties that would be generated.

He made positive suggestions asking for more information about the use of drugs in terminal distress, calling for better care of the dying and for support for the work of the London Medical Group and the Institute of Religion and Medicine in the ethical training of doctors.

LORD AILWYN said public opinion was moving in support of euthanasia. Why should we be more merciful to animals than to human beings? His views were reinforced by a visit to an old people's hospital. Those who believed in an after-life should agree that a suffering mortal be given the right to be wafted painlessly into it.

THE EARL OF LONGFORD said that life was not ours to dispose of. In answer to the argument that if suicide was not illegal one should not object to suicide by proxy, he said that we do not approve of suicide, we merely did not prosecute because of our sympathy for the sufferer. Suicide pacts could not be justified. We must assume that the doctor is in his right mind, so his participation is not excused. He confirmed that there was no objection to the use of drugs to relieve pain, even at the risk of shortening life as a secondary or side effect, and he asserted strongly that it was wrong to maintain the vegetative sort of life which had been referred to.

Voluntary euthanasia would lead inevitably to compulsory euthanasia. 'Once you abandon the idea that life is sacred . . . I do not see where you are likely to stop.' The Bill would be paving the way to a new attitude 'the consequences of which would be calamitous'. It initiated the thesis that we should dispatch ourselves when we were no longer useful; the question 'What is the use of me?' would carry widespread terror. If it were fairly established as part of our national consciousness, old people would suffer agonies as to whether they were cumbering the ground and ought to be put away. To pass the Bill would mean approving an attitude of life and death 'opposed to some of the foundations of human society and some of the truest instincts of the human race'.

LORD SOPER said 'though I am in favour of euthanasia . . . I cannot support this Bill'. The matter needed deeper thought. He did not want the matter to be left to the doctors: this was cowardly escapism on the part of people trying to spare themselves the painful trouble of deciding on the principles. It was dangerous for people to be expected to play God.

Life, to be sacrosanct, must be self-conscious life, for it was not sacrosanct in animals or vegetables, so we should have no hesitation in allowing patients to die who were only organically alive. He appreciated that many of the old and dying clung to life. Nor was suicide always immoral, and he quoted not only Captain Oates but Father Damien who 'induced death by going to a leper colony knowing that sooner or later he would contract the disease', but he rejoined with the quotation 'Greater love hath no man than this, that he lay down his life for his friends'.

In his view every man had the right to give up his own life, to choose to be allowed to die. But he also has a perfect right to ask others to stay out of the way in the exercise of his choice. He hoped though that if he were in an irreparable condition causing suffering to those who had to care for him, he would have the courage and the intelligence to opt to give his life; and if he did, to ask the medical profession to let him die. He hoped they would give him medicaments to alleviate pain; but he would not ask them to kill him.

LORD THURLOW said the Bill would be easily misinterpreted or misused. It was not possible to provide proper safeguards once you accepted the principle. We could easily find ourselves deciding that others had no right to live. Did we want the distinction of being the first country to initiate such legislation?

It was dangerous in principle as well as in practice. It would become more difficult to teach students when to stop medication. What was needed was discussion and concern for people.

Euthanasia was a negative approach. He spoke of the advances in geriatrics and in particular of St Christopher's of which he was Chairman. At that hospice five hundred people had died in two years—none of them in pain. Most had been alert to the end.

'I should like to die' was a cry of despair from a depressed patient needing treatment or attention to his problems; in few was it a definite decision. He pleaded for more geriatric units. Euthanasia was a confession of failure. It could also lead to feelings of guilt—would the families be able to bear the decisions? LORD PLATT thought that many of the objections were just the points that made the Bill attractive. He considered situations in which he said 'a certain amount of euthanasia is already used'. If a terminal cancer patient developed pneumonia should antibiotics be given to cure the pneumonia? Or severe accident cases with no hope of recovery of useful conscious life, who were kept alive by artificial respirators etc.—in these cases did we not believe in euthanasia? The possibility of switching off these arrangements at a prearranged time would put new power into the hands of the medical profession. This might be morally and legally inconvenient, but was an inescapable result of scientific progress —and was essential in, for example, transplant surgery.

His only doubts were as to whether it was necessary to make laws when a good deal of understanding already existed and as to whether the Bill was good enough to go on to a further stage for further consideration of the objectives. He concluded that it should. Referring back to Lord Brock's quotation from B.M.A. decisions he thought they were not consistent with the views of many medical people today.

LORD BEAUMONT OF WHITLEY claimed the right to end his life when he wanted to do so. When he most wanted to exercise this he might not be in a position to do so and that was why he should be able to decide beforehand and thereby ask the doctors to help in executing his decision.

LORD CLIFFORD OF CHUDLEIGH referred to the continuous improvement in drugs. This argued against the Bill. The Bill was very disturbing to the elderly. The old who felt a burden needed the protection of society, not an added weapon in the armoury of suicide. Depressives were among those who might sign a declaration and he quoted Lord Horder's reference to 'misère' in the 1950 debate.

Lord Clifford told an anecdote: once on falling with his horse he was surprised when his wife attended to the horse rather than to him, but, as a friend reminded him later, she might have had to shoot the horse.

He concluded that the Bill was medically unnecessary, psychologically dangerous and ethically wrong.

THE EARL OF LISTOWEL asserted there was more public support for euthanasia than in the past and referred to the Suicide Act. There was a stronger ethical case for euthanasia than for suicide. It would enlarge the area of individual freedom.

Many doctors practised euthanasia already. If doctors were prepared to administer euthanasia themselves why should they not do it on behalf of society. It was unfair to expect them to act on their professional judgement regardless of the criminal law. It was also unfair to the patient that his right to death should be put in jeopardy by the chance of having a doctor who objected to euthanasia.

LORD ARCHIBALD was greatly influenced by the experience of his mother, who suffered a vegetative existence for two years. He supported the principle of voluntary euthanasia.

LORD GRENFELL feared that there many who could be persuaded to sign without understanding fully what they were doing. The rules were unfair to doctors: whatever a doctor did there would be someone to say he was wrong. The Bill condoned the procuring of murder and the abetting of suicide. Once the Bill was passed, further extensions would be almost inevitable.

VISCOUNT WAVERLEY said that like the Abortion Bill the present Bill displayed an imperfect understanding of existing medical practice. Over the centuries the profession had evolved serviceable ethics: legal rigidity should not be substituted for medical discretion. Clause 8 was crucial: if medical practice fulfilled the requirements of that Clause, the other clauses were superfluous —and to his mind it did, though not at the patient's 'request'.

Such a request would virtually be never forthcoming and if it was left to the request of the patient the desired relief would seldom be given.

THE EARL OF HUNTINGDON quoted a tragic case of a girl of fourteen or fifteen years of age. He did not think doctors could be bribed or suborned, but the responsibility of life and death was already in their hands. The Bill guarded against the dangers, for there would be no rush decision and one of the doctors concerned must be of consultant status. He explained the lack of demand for euthanasia in terms of the lack of facility for it.

LORD BALERNO thought the soul did not leave the body only when the last vestiges of life had ceased, and there was no justification for keeping the body alive when the spirit no longer survived.

LORD RITCHIE-CALDER agreed with that view, as a non-Christian. He quoted the experience of three aged aunts: one had been hopelessly paralysed since the age of two, and the other two spent the whole of their lives looking after her. Sooner or later Parliament would have to consider the factors which science was introducing into the topic.

LORD POLTIMORE spoke briefly against the Bill, mainly on the grounds of the fallibility of the medical profession.

LADY SUMMERSKILL said the matter could not be thought of only in theoretical terms: the problems were essentially human and some of the assumptions of the Bill were naive. Suicide involved only the individual concerned, but this Bill involved every one suffering from incurable disease.

She had never been asked by a patient for an overdose. However ill a man was, life was still sweet. Where, she asked, did the demand for this Bill come from?

The Bill made it clear that the declarant must be sane, but the chronically sick were not lucid, albeit not mentally sick. Such a one might sign a declaration and then wait thirty days for death. Who was to tell him that he was doomed? His rights would have to be brought to his notice by somebody. Perhaps a tiny minority might opt for dismissal, but the majority would suffer intensely from the knowledge that they could release their relations from a burden, or that their family was divided on the subject. In over-crowded homes pressures could be unspoken, and there would be no need for positive urging : the old man occupying a room needed by one of the children would in fact be under pressure, and might develop a sense of guilt and sign his own death warrant. Then, feeling better, he would revoke it—and the horror of subtle persuasion would begin again.

The doctor could ask the nurse to administer a dose : the nurse, who might be a young girl just qualified, was chosen as the execu-tioner. 'Who could have been so un-thinking as to put that into this Bill?' If the doctor or the nurse at the last moment refused to give the lethal dose, there would be a gruesome search for replacements. The only people she could think of as qualified executioners were those dedicated to this particular purpose—and she suggested that the Committee of the Euthanasia Society should make their own choice : no one who supported the Bill could say 'This hand will not hold the dagger.'

Futhermore, there was the question of statutory method for killing. What was the kindest method? 'Here we hang, but in the United States they . . . kill their criminals with an electric chair.' And what would the death certificate say? For example, cancer might be a contributory cause, but the immediate cause could be morphia poisoning.

THE EARL FERRERS was against the Bill for two reasons. He dis-agreed with euthanasia in principle, and he was sure that the principle of voluntary euthanasia would give way to a more general application of the practice.

The Bill had an emotional appeal, but one had to look to the effect of the law on society as a whole. It would be wrong to terminate the lives of others, even within limits.

There were two types of pressure, active and passive. Even the active might show a genuine desire to help, though even here the motives might be mixed. He did not believe, as Lord Raglan suggested, that the Bill took care of the unscrupulous, for the unscrupulous could act in a scrupulous way. As to the passive pressures, he visualized the horrible situation of the patient know-ing that he was a liability to everyone and thinking—perhaps erroneously—that his relations would be happier with him out of the way.

VISCOUNT BARRINGTON summarized his opposition to the Bill by saying that it was not practical, and his opposition to the principle by saying that it was wicked. He did not think that euthanasia could be voluntary.

LORD STRABOLGI spoke against the Bill as the Honorary President of Aegis. Elderly people might sign away their lives without realizing it. It was paradoxical that one of the accepted arguments against the death penalty—that an innocent man would be dead before his innocence was discovered—should be ignored in relation to this Bill. The Bill was a dangerous precedent and could lead to the authorised killing of lunatics, and others.

THE BISHOP OF EXETER (Dr Mortimer) said the principle of the Bill was assisted suicide, and was quite contrary to Christianity. The compassion which sought to relieve the sufferings of a few would end in causing more suffering than it relieved. There would be a great fear of entering a geriatric hospital. The true compassion would be to press for further research and better attention to geriatric care.

LORD SEGAL emphasised the fallibility of human judgement. The doctors were content with the present arrangements. Every doctor had to hearken to his patient's plea and then to decide the issue for himself. Permissive legislation would not lighten the burden. He had to struggle with his own conscience, and would prefer to continue under existing conditions.

LORD MERTHYR suggested that the Bill be referred to a Select Committee.

LORD FERRIER agreed, as a supporter of the Bill. He was worried by the lack of disputation on the ethical and medical aspects of death control. He was also worried about the implications for life assurance.

VISCOUNT ST DAVIDS said he would support the Bill if it were referred to a Select Committee, but not otherwise.

LORD RAGLAN summed up very briefly, and accepted the suggestion of a Select Committee.

THE EARL OF CORK AND ORRERY declined to accept Lord

Merthyr's suggestion, and after summing up pressed the matter to a Division.

There voted : for the Bill 40; against the Bill 61. (Lord Raglan having accepted the suggestion of a Select Committee, Lord St Davids voted for the Bill, but it is not known whether any other Lords voted for the Bill for that reason.)

A Further Bill Rejected—Unseen

The fourth and most recent debate on the subject was in the House of Commons on 7 April 1970.[5] This debate took place under what is known as 'The Ten-Minute Rule'. This rule allows a short debate, not on a Bill, but on a motion for leave to introduce a Bill. Where leave is refused, as in this case, the Bill itself is not published as a Parliamentary paper, though its supporters may of course publish it privately if they wish. The Ten-Minute Rule allows only one speech from the member seeking leave to introduce the Bill, and one speech from an opponent of the motion.

On this occasion Dr Hugh Gray (Yarmouth) was asking for leave to 'bring in a Bill to make lawful administration of euthanasia at the request of the recipient'.

DR GRAY began by citing the three occasions when the subject had been discussed in the House of Lords, referring in particular to the defeat on Second Reading by 61 votes to 40 of Lord Raglan's Bill in 1969. His argument in favour of the Bill rested on the contention that the choice of life or death should always be with the individual concerned, and that the things that happened to him should be in accordance with his values and not the values of others. This choice at the moment rested with the doctors who broadly fell into three groups : they either practised a certain amount of euthanasia already (for example, by withholding drugs in cases of very serious illness), or else they did 'not strive officiously to keep alive' the patient according to their own humane values, or thirdly they held that life had an absolute value which in no circumstances must be ended. The views of this third group in Dr Gray's opinion offended against the terms

[5] Hansard, H. of C., vol 799, cols 252-258.

of individual liberty which required that the choice should rest with the individual.

He went on to draw an analogy between his present proposal and the fact that since 1961 it had become lawful to take one's own life. The existing situation regarding euthanasia meant that a person involved in an accident who did not wish to be kept alive might be cared for by a doctor with the absolute values of the third group or again, a person with these absolute values ran the risk of being cared for by a doctor who took a different view.

His solution was to give statutory effect to an individual declaration either for or against euthanasia which would accompany a person's medical record. He took Lord Platt's definition of euthanasia, namely, the termination of life at the request of the individual for the purpose of avoiding unnecessary suffering in the last extremity, and suggested that the declaration might take the form proposed by Lord Raglan in his Bill (see Appendix). But, he explained, any declaration would be voluntary, made in accordance with a person's own values. Provision would be made for its renewal and possibly for retention in a central registry. He rejected as 'paternalistic' the suggestion made in *The Times* that the choice was better left to the humane values of doctors and hoped that the House would grant him the opportunity to bring in his Bill to enable the subject to be discussed at greater length. The principle at stake was one of individual choice which as an adult he wanted to be able to make.

MR NORMAN ST JOHN STEVAS (Chelmsford) rose to speak in reply against the Motion. He congratulated the proposer of the Motion on the manner of presenting his case, involving as it did the important issues of life and death.

One of the great achievements of modern medical science had been to conquer disease and illness and thereby increase the expectancy of life in a way no other age had seen. But these achievements themselves posed real and complex problems as more people were surviving in a state where their powers and faculties had waned or wasted away. The response of those in favour of euthanasia, no doubt dictated by compassion and humane motives, was to put people at their request out of their misery. Equally, however, Mr Stevas was convinced that it was neither compassionate nor humane to facilitate euthanasia as proposed by the Bill.

Fundamentally, his objection to the proposals was religious. As an heir to the Judaeo-Christian tradition, he believed that ultimately God the creator, and not man the created, had the disposal of human life. That being said it had to be recognized that one of the hallmarks of man's humanity was his freedom to choose, to transcend the limits of his nature. Advancing technology by putting more and more power into man's hands created a tension between these two principles and the resolution of that tension would determine the future of humanity.

His suggested solution to the problem was to turn to the moral values of society which were both its inherited and developing wisdom. The proposal before the House would offend the principle that no individual had the right to dispose of the life of another and that life could only be taken in extreme cases at the hands of the State. To do away with this principle would expose society to a whole variety of dangers. The burden of proof that the proposed change would not undermine respect for life lay with those advocating it; he did not believe this burden had been discharged by Dr Gray.

Mr Stevas continued by describing as 'inadequate' the analysis that what was involved was simply a transfer of choice from doctor to patient. A doctor, whatever his views, had a duty to preserve life. This duty was the basis of the patient-doctor relationship but it did not mean that life was to be prolonged at any cost. There was clearly a moral distinction between giving a pain-killing drug knowing that it may or will shorten life and giving a drug with the direct intention to kill. The safeguard of that distinction was in the standards of the medical profession, supported by the law.

He ended by referring to the agonising moral pressure to which the Bill might well expose old people, anxious to relieve families and friends of the burden they imposed. The trouble with the Bill was that it offered a simple solution to problems of the highest complexity. What was needed was an effort to enable those dying of old age or disease to die in dignity and peace, to assuage the inner misery and loneliness of such people and to allow them to achieve an interior peace in reconciling themselves to life and death.

The Question on the Motion was put, and was negatived without a division.

The Changing Argument

The debate in 1969—and to some extent the brief debate in 1970—as compared with the earlier debates, reflected three changes in the background to the controversy. First, there was the improved power of medical skill to relieve suffering. This was mentioned by several speakers, but no very great emphasis was put upon it.

Secondly, there was the increased power of medical science to sustain some form of life in patients hopelessly near death. Speakers on both sides in 1969 referred to this aspect, and to the right—if not duty—of a doctor to withdraw extraordinary means[6] of resuscitation etc, at a time indicated by his clinical judgement. The supporters of the Bill classified such withdrawal as euthanasia, claiming that as it was ethically acceptable, it should be legalised. Other speakers realised that no change in the law was necessary: a doctor who, in appropriate circumstances, withdrew such extraordinary means, would not be in peril of the law. The supporters of the Bill, by calling such withdrawal euthanasia, were able to give it the same name as the obvious cases of 'suicide by proxy'. Thus, by a false exemplar, they made their case sound plausible. It is clear from the speeches against the Bill that not all of its opponents had spotted that fallacy.

The third difference was the passing of the Suicide Act 1961. This was referred to by many speakers, some saying that the 'right' to commit suicide was at its most valuable when the patient was least able to use it for himself, and that he should therefore have the services of a doctor to do it for him, others

[6] The significance of the term 'extraordinary means' is explained in Chapter VII.

maintaining that there was no comparison between the circumstances in which people normally committed suicide and those in which they would ask for euthanasia.

The 1969 debate showed that many peers were impressed by the report issued by the Central Ethical Committee of the British Medical Association condemning euthanasia, and that many had a clear understanding of the hidden pressures which might affect the signing of declarations etc, and of the psychological consequences on those encouraging patients to sign, and those charged with the administration of euthanasia. This does not seem to have been so clear to speakers in the 1936 and 1950 debates.

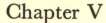

Chapter V

The law and the legal implications of euthanasia

Introduction: The Current Law of Homicide

The commandment traditionally rendered as 'Thou shalt not kill' has been faithfully reflected in English law. To take the life of another deliberately is the crime of murder. Deliberate action intended to shorten life and having this effect is no less murder although the death of the victim appeared to be inevitable from other causes within a foreseeable future. Until 1965 the more heinous types of murder carried the death penalty. The penalty for all classes of murder is now imprisonment for life although the average sentence served by murderers is much less. Causing the death of another by violent or negligent conduct but without the intent to kill is manslaughter, for which the punishment lies in the discretion of the Court and is variable within wide limits. Cases described as 'mercy killing' are either murder or manslaughter.

The child in the womb is protected under the law. The offence of child destruction consists in deliberately causing to die an infant capable of being born alive. Evidence of twenty-eight weeks pregnancy is prima facie proof that the infant was capable of being born alive (The Infant Life (Preservation) Act, 1929). The Abortion Act, 1967, permits termination of pregnancy if two doctors consider that its continuance would carry risk to the life of the woman or injury to her health or that of her children; or that there is a substantial risk that her child would be born with serious abnormality. Apart from these circumstances, involving an expert assessment of medical matters, the law against abortion and the Infant Life Act of 1929 stand unimpaired.

Modern amendments of the law have enabled juries to substitute verdicts of manslaughter for murder. Thus provocation of sufficient degree, even when an intent to kill existed, will permit this course. A jury may also reduce the verdict on the ground of diminished responsibility, i.e. a finding that the accused was suffering from such abnormality of mind, however arising, as substantially impaired his mental responsibility for his conduct. The law has also in this century looked more kindly on the mother who kills her child. If a woman wilfully kills a child less than a year old, but at the time the balance of her mind was disturbed in consequence of giving birth, she is guilty not of murder but of infanticide punishable as for manslaughter.

The common law did not permit a person to take his own life and attempted suicide was a crime. This was altered by the Suicide Act, 1961. But it remains a serious crime for a person to incite or assist another to commit suicide or to attempt to do so.

Hence it is plain that the attitude of the law remains unflinchingly opposed to the taking of another's life and will punish those who offend with the sternest penalties which the justice of the case requires and the will of Parliament places at its disposal. The protection of the law is given to life, whether it is long or short, sweet or bitter.

The Meaning of Euthanasia

The proponents of euthanasia claim that it is desirable in certain circumstances and ought to be made lawful, for a person deliberately to kill another. 'Euthanasia' means literally a 'good' or 'easy' death. On the lips of the would-be reformers it means a deliberate killing effected painlessly. It may for them also mean a death not intentionally brought about but foreseen by the medical man in charge as a possible consequence of the administration of drugs designed to relieve pain or distress, or of the withdrawal of extraordinary means of maintaining life in a patient who would otherwise expire. Such circumstances are not infrequently encountered in hospital practice. They are dealt with in accordance with the conscience and good sense of the medical attendants. They differ from euthanasia in its morbid sense in that no action is taken with the intention or wish to terminate life. 'If the first purpose of medicine—the restoration of health—can no longer be achieved, there is still much for the doctor to do and he is entitled to do all that is proper and necessary to relieve pain and suffering even if the measures he takes may incidentally shorten life. . . . But it remains the law that no doctor has the right to cut off life deliberately.' (Mr Justice Devlin (now Lord Devlin) summing up in R -v- Adams, Central Criminal Court, 1957.) Hence the law is clear, and consistent with medical practice. The test lies not in the outcome of what the doctor directs, but in the intent with which he gives the direction. No change in the law is necessary to authorise that which doctors find to be in accordance with their own ethical standards; and the term 'euthanasia' should be confined to its morbid meaning. A change in the law which permitted them 'to cut off life deliberately' in any circumstances would be a change inconsistent with the whole tenor of medical practice, and a change which the profession as a whole neither demands nor desires.

The Voluntary Euthanasia Bill rejected by the House of Lords on 25 March 1969 included a clause (8) which provided 'for the removal of doubt' that a patient believed to be suffering from a fatal condition should be 'entitled' to be administered whatever quantity of drugs was required to keep him free from pain and, if he wished, continuously unconscious. There is no doubt about the present legal position. A patient is not 'entitled' to any particular form of treatment. He may ask, and the doctor may accede to his wishes, but to say that he is 'entitled' would be to impose a corresponding duty to provide. This would be a novel and objectionable conception in medicine. If it were admitted in principle, it would be but a short step to say that the patient's relatives were entitled to dictate to the doctor to what extent the patient would be relieved from pain. The final decision as to how and to what extent pain or distress should be relieved must rest with the medical attendant, even in the case of a patient thought to be dying, just as it rests with the doctor to be the final arbiter as regards any other form of medical treatment.

The Proposed Procedure for Euthanasia

The other provisions of the 1969 Bill may be taken to indicate the views of the sponsors of euthanasia as to the circumstances in which it should be legalised and the safeguards that ought to be attached to ensure that any expressed desire of a person to have his life prematurely terminated represented a genuine and continuing wish. The circumstances prescribed were that a person had made a declaration of subscription to a code set out in the scheduled form and that two doctors (one being a consultant) had certified in writing that the patient, being then of full age, appeared to them to be suffering from an irremediable condition. 'Irremediable condition' was said to mean a serious physical illness or impairment reasonably thought in the patient's case to be incurable and expected to cause him severe distress or render him incapable of rational existence.

The definition of 'irremediable condition' is of supreme importance. It enshrines the root conception of the Bill in that it implies the assertion that certain states of ill-health are so unbearable as to make life not worth living and that a person in such a state should be entitled to enlist the help of a doctor to bring his life to a close. The breadth of the definition is noteworthy. It does not depend on any expert belief that the 'condition' is terminal. Since the definition is wide enough to cover the loss of a limb no such requirement is to be expected. The use of the word 'physical' merits attention. In ordinary lay understanding (from which legal interpretation is not far removed) the term denotes some observable damage to, or deterioration in, the structure or working of the bodily frame and is to be contrasted with a mental illness recognisable only from the person's actions, manner or words, pointing to a lack or disorientation of his intellectual faculties. Unless this distinction is sought to be made the word 'physical' is surplusage. But it is envisaged, seemingly, that a 'physical illness' may give rise to incapacity for 'rational existence'. It is undoubtedly true that some physical illnesses in the sense described are the product or concomitant of brain damage or deterioration; but what of those whose minds are defective, diseased or decayed but whose mental condition is not betrayed by any apparent bodily sign? Would senile degeneration or other disorders of the mind not overtly affecting physical capacities fall within the phrase 'physical illness or impairment'? The general medical view may be that practically all disordered states of mind are referable to detectable or diagnosable physical abnormalities of the brain. Is this opinion intended to govern the meaning of 'physical illness'?

The definition presents several other serious points of inadequacy and uncertainty. For example, the qualification that the condition should be 'expected to cause (the patient) severe distress' ignores the possibility of treatment alleviating his distress. This omission removes almost all effect from the word 'irremediable'. There is no indication at what point of time the expected distress or incapacity for rational existence should be anticipated so as to satisfy the definition. The difficulty in giving meaning to 'rational existence' is ignored. It is a term unknown to the law. 'Rational' means 'guided by reason'. There are some people whose conduct at many points in their lives may be said to be 'irrational'. There are many whose behaviour or thinking is not governed by reason in respect of particular subjects. Is any expected level of departure from the supposed norm to be regarded as exhibiting incapacity for 'rational existence'? If not, to what extent must incapacity of this character be expected to affect the future life of the patient? A person might be capable of living a happy and placid life as a hospital patient while quite incapable of sensibly running a business. To what extent does capacity for 'rational existence' depend on power to communicate, of which a grievously ill person may be wholly or substantially bereft?

As will later be urged persons suffering from mental disorder should be regarded as incapable of making a valid declaration. On the assumption that the reference to incapacity for 'rational existence' would involve a genuine prognosis of some severe form of mental disability—albeit undefined and not to be measured by any recognised criteria—what assurance would there be that the expectation had not already been realised? Persons within this part of the definition should not therefore be competent to make a declaration, or to confirm one previously made.

The declaration incorporated a statement of adherence to the conditions which the two doctors have to assess and a request for euthanasia if they are satisfied. It also contained a request that if such conditions exist no active steps should be taken and no resuscitatory techniques used to prolong life. Would this apply to supervening conditions such as pneumonia? There was no requirement that at the time of making the declaration the declarant should be of full age or free from mental disorder.

In an attempt to avoid the objectionable death-bed formalities and safeguards proposed in an earlier Bill, introduced in 1936, the promoters of the 1969 Bill turned to an advance declaration which was marked by the deficiency in its protective formalities. Two witnesses were required to attest the execution of the document; a device presumably drawn from the law governing the execution of a will. But witnesses to a will merely verify the signature of the testator. They are not expected to know the contents of the document and need not even know that it is a will. They do not verify the testamentary capacity of the testator, although if this is challenged they may have pertinent evidence to give. The witnesses to the declaration were required to testify that the declarant 'appeared to appreciate (the) significance' of the declaration and their belief that 'it (was) made by his own wish'. Such assurances possess only the most superficial value. No sound judgement could be formed on such matters unless the witnesses themselves made an intelligent study of the whole document and thus understood to what the declarant was putting his signature. An intelligent witness who attempted to do so might well find his understanding to be restricted on account of the obscurities of meaning already mentioned.

The classes of person competent to act as attesting witnesses was left, with other important matters including any 'he may think fit to prescribe', to be covered by Regulations to be made by the Minister for Social Services. This unique omnibus provision was a pointer to the difficulties of the subject which the draftsmen preferred to shelve rather than to meet.

The Bill provided that a declaration should come into force thirty days after execution and should remain in force for three years; if re-executed within twelve months preceding its expiry it should remain in force for life. This provision plainly contemplated the possibility of many years interval between execution of the declaration and execution of the declarant, during which his readiness to have his death hastened might cease. He was therefore given power to revoke, by destruction or defacement of the document, effected personally or by his order. Until the important matter of responsibility for custody of the declaration had been determined by the Minister the working of these provisions was uncertain. But it is fair to say that they appear to be very restrictive since they involve either retrieving the document or relying on the holder to destroy or cancel it. However, a safeguard was introduced in favour of a 'mentally responsible patient'. The physician in charge was required to 'ascertain to his reasonable satisfaction that the declaration and all steps proposed to be taken under it accord with the patient's wishes'. This requirement cast on a single doctor the duty to assess 'mental responsibility' in a unique context; and seemingly left patients thought to lack 'mental responsibility' powerless to avert the consequences of having signed a declaration. The Bill was silent as to the meaning of 'mental responsibility' and its relationship to incapacity for 'rational existence'.

'Mental responsibility' possesses the slender merit of being a phrase known to the law. Under the Homicide Act 1957 it is open to a jury in a murder case to return a verdict of manslaughter on the ground that (as already above mentioned) the accused was suffering from such abnormality of mind as substantially impaired his mental responsibility for his 'acts . . . in doing . . . the killing'. The finding is that of the jury. The approved direction by the judge to the jury is that the term 'mental responsibility' requires consideration of the extent to which the mind of the accused was answerable for his physical acts including consideration of the extent of his ability to exercise will-power over his acts. Thus the jury's attention is focused on the accused's state of mind at the time of, and solely with reference to, the act of killing. 'Mental responsibility' is a meaningless idea except in relation to such positive conduct. It is wholly inept to use it in respect of a helpless bed patient. 'Responsibility' is not to be found *in vacuo*. It can only exist or be refuted in reference to something done or omitted to be done. If the intention was to relieve the physician in charge of any obligation to canvass the current wishes of a person believed to be suffering from some recognised form of mental disorder this should have been made plain, instead of being concealed by a novel and empty phrase. The uncovering of such an intention would justifiably lead to a demand that the existence of the disorder should be confirmed by an independent practitioner of consultant status. If the true intention was to leave the judgement of 'mental responsibility' to a single doctor unhampered by any indication as to what it means, then it becomes apparent that persons who had once signed a declaration and exhibited any sign of mental disorientation in illness might be despatched from life without being given an opportunity to disclose their real wishes.

Essential Procedural Requirements for Euthanasia

If, contrary to established and deeply-rooted principles, the intentional killing of another is to be sanctioned by the law provided it is done with the authority of the victim, the most scrupulous care must be taken to ensure that the authority has been truly given and effectively subsists. Only those who are fully competent to conduct all transactions under the law should be viewed as capable to give the requisite authority. Hence minors and persons who are mentally disordered within the meaning of the Mental Health Act 1959 should be excluded. The former cannot make a will; the testamentary capacity of the latter must be suspect. It would indeed be anomalous if those who lack legal competence to dispose of their property could nevertheless will their life away. Consideration of the position of persons of disordered mind provokes the question whether, if a period of mental disorder follows the making of a declaration, the declaration should remain in force. The reasons to the contrary are that for the period in question the intention expressed in the declaration is unlikely to have been consciously maintained; and any apparent assent to the original intention expressed while seriously ill would be tainted by the possibility that the person had not wholly recovered from, or had suffered a recurrence of, mental disorder. These reasons lead to the conclusion that supervening mental disorder should automatically operate to revoke a previous declaration. The difficulty of ensuring that such a rule would be respected in practice is acknowledged. But although mental incapacity should be regarded as negativing a previous desire to submit to euthanasia it may not prevent a declarant forming a wish to cancel his declaration and accordingly a purported revocation should not be open to doubt on account of his then state of mind.

Safeguards of much greater value than any hinted at in the Bill should be required to attend the making of the declaration. No person related by blood or marriage and no person who might benefit directly or indirectly by the death should be competent witnesses. Only independent persons of public or professional status should be capable to act as witnesses. Their duty to verify the declarant's understanding of the contents of the document should be authoritatively and explicitly prescribed. This is particularly necessary in the case of hospital patients whose normal capacities may be reduced by suffering and whose mental faculties may be clouded by depression.

It may be reasonably contended that power to revoke a declaration should be at least as liberal as is the power to revoke a will. A will may be revoked by a later will or formally executed instrument without any tampering with the original text. It is also revoked by marriage because marriage creates a fresh situation with new claims on testamentary benevolence. Marriage may also induce a new outlook on a previous desire to submit to a premature extinction of life. A wish to live a full seven years so as to avoid estate duty on a gift to a wife is an obvious example; a wish to survive until the partner is old enough to receive the widow's pension is another; and others, less mercenary, may arise. The gravity of the matter calls for an unqualified right to revoke a declaration by any explicit form of statement to be respected by any person to whom it is communicated and passed on to all others concerned. A person should not run the risk of entering hospital for a serious condition in the shadow of a declaration to which he has not maintained his full assent. The safeguard to be found in the duty of the 'physician in charge' might prove illusory if the patient was deemed not to be 'mentally responsible' and furthermore the patient's condition might make it impossible for him to convey his real wishes. But again the administrative difficulties in the way of ensuring observance of the revocation not apparent from the absence, or the defacement, of the declaration must be recognised.

From Voluntary to Involuntary Euthanasia

The need for safeguards is accepted by the proponents of euthanasia—safeguards against unconsidered declarations by persons not in a fit state of mind to deal with so serious a matter and to negative the possibility that a change of heart on the subject should pass unnoticed. It is contended that the devices proposed were quite inadequate to meet these needs and that the procedure set out in the Bill would produce instances of involuntary euthanasia. If adequate safeguards such as have been discussed were to be introduced, it is admittedly open to doubt whether they would be workable in practice.

It is not without significance that the word 'voluntary' featured in the title of the Bill. It recognises the possibility of involuntary euthanasia while purporting to avoid any such proposal. It is difficult to avoid the conclusion that the sponsors of the Bill would find only a small gap to bridge between their current ideas and involuntary euthanasia applied to the grossly abnormal child on the authority of the parents, to those of permanently unbalanced mind and to the severe geriatric cases—all in the supposed overriding interest of society as a whole.

The width of the definition of 'irremediable condition' gives substance to this anticipation. If Parliament were to declare that such ill-defined conditions of ill-health justified calling for destruction at the hand of another the value of the individual's right to life would be materially debased. Very critical comment has already been made of the phrases 'rational existence' and 'mental responsibility'. Their obscurity of meaning is so patent that no conscientious medical man could act in confidence on his own interpretation. But doctors lacking in scruple could make of them what they pleased. It would be objectionable in the highest degree that some, perhaps many, persons would have to succumb to premature killing before the law was given an opportunity to pronounce authoritatively upon the true meaning of these phrases, if indeed it is possible to give them any precise meaning.

Finally a feature of the proposed procedure must be noted : a declaration made in illness would remain inoperative for thirty days after which time it might be implemented immediately. There was nothing in the Bill to exclude the jurisdiction of the coroner and it is certainly to be expected that a death intentionally brought about would receive his attention. It would fall within the class of 'unnatural' deaths for the purpose of the Coroners Act 1887 and would have to be notified. The Coroner would require to be satisfied that the procedural requirements of the new law, which alone could justify the extinction of life, had been scrupulously observed. But if the death occurred on the twenty-ninth day it could easily be ascribed to natural causes, although it had in fact been induced, and the interest of the coroner would be excluded. This possibility emphasises the undesirability of requiring the medical profession, contrary to the natural instincts of their calling, to become death-dispensing agents.

Chapter VI

The ethics of euthanasia

This chapter seeks to examine the general ethical aspects of euthanasia on a basis which we believe will be acceptable to those who do not subscribe to a formal faith, notwithstanding that many of our arguments are drawn from lines of thought traditional in Christian philosophy.

As has been pointed out in the introductory chapter, much of the discussion has been blurred by the vague use of the term 'euthanasia'. There is no ethical merit in prolonging the process of dying, but it is false logic to equate the active termination of life with allowing someone to die peacefully without extraordinary efforts at resuscitation. Much stir was caused some time ago when instructions were issued in a hospital that patients above a certain age should not be resuscitated; these instructions were misguided because they were given as a general ruling, without consideration of individual circumstances, which can be judged only by the doctor attending the patient at the relevant time.

It would appear from the debate on the Voluntary Euthanasia Bill in the House of Lords in March 1969[1] that even a man of the learning of the Bishop of Durham could be misled by the ambiguity of the term euthanasia, for he said that one of the contexts in which this question arose was that of keeping people alive by highly artificial means. We must emphasise again: to abstain from keeping people artificially alive by such means is

[1] Hansard, H. of L., 25 March 1969, vol 300, col 1180.

not euthanasia in the sense of the Bill. The indefinite prolonga-
tion of life when the patient has no prospect of ever again being
able to maintain his own life, or no prospect of leading a life
rewarding to himself even with artificial aid, is in fact a travesty
of sound medicine: it makes a mockery both of life and of the
process of dying.

There is a further clear distinction between using means
for the relief of suffering which may, as a secondary result, shorten
life, and actively ending life. Here the guide is the principle
known as the principle of double effect. It is a principle commonly misunderstood, but one which in fact guides doctors whenever the problem of undesirable side effects arises with any treatment. And not only doctors: very many of our acts have more
than one foreseeable consequence; if one foreseeable consequence
is undesirable we have to weigh up whether or not to do the act
we have in mind. There are four criteria:

   (i)   the act itself must be morally good, or at least neutral;
  (ii)   the purpose must be to achieve the good consequence, the
           bad consequence being only a side effect;
 (iii)   the good effect must not be achieved by way of the bad,
           but both must result from the same act;
 (iv)   the bad result must not be so serious as to outweigh the
           advantage of the good result.

In practice these criteria can involve difficulties in judgement,
but the ignoring of these criteria does not ease any problems; it
merely permits evasion.

The use of medicaments with the intention of relieving pain
is good, and if by repeated pain-relief the patient's resistance is
lowered and he dies earlier than he would otherwise have done,
this is a side effect which may well be acceptable. More often
than not life will not be shortened in this way, because the benefit of rest and sleep and an untroubled mind will do the patient
more good than heavy sedation will do him harm.[2] On the other
hand, to give an overdose *with the intention that the patient*

---

[2] K. F. M. Pole, *Handbook for the Catholic Nurse*, Robert Hale Ltd.,
(1964).

should never wake up is morally wrong. It is killing. The protection of life is not only the concern of the churches, it is deeply entrenched in law. It was one of the accepted arguments against the death penalty that a man might be mistakenly convicted of a crime. Essentially the same consideration must be given to any man who has done no wilful harm, and Kamisar rightly put the question, 'What is the need for euthanasia which leads us to tolerate the mistakes, the very fatal mistakes, that will inevitably occur?'[3]

This principle of double effect has long been acknowledged as valid by the Catholic Church : although it has only been strictly formulated as a general principle in the last century or so, its origins go back to the time of St Thomas Aquinas, who stated the principle clearly in connection with self-defence. Thus the authors of the Euthanasia Society's *Plan for Voluntary Euthanasia* (1962) are wide of the mark when they write : *'Even the Roman Catholic Church has recently agreed* that where a human life is ending in great suffering it is the doctor's duty to relieve that suffering, even although the means taken may shorten life.'[4] It is blurring the all-important clear definition of the term euthanasia when later on the same authors state : 'If that policy shortens the patient's life, even by a few hours, the doctor is, in fact, practising euthanasia, although not strictly *voluntary* euthanasia.'[5] What the doctor is doing is to relieve his patient's suffering. As a secondary effect he may be securing for his patient euthanasia in the literal sense of an easy death, but he is very certainly *not killing* his patient, that is, he is not practising euthanasia in the sense for which legislation is sought.

In the foreword to a recently published book on euthanasia the Earl of Listowel writes : 'We can now urge that the moral right to a dignified and merciful death, from which the legal right will eventually flow, should be enshrined in the Universal Declaration of Human Rights adopted in 1949 by the General

---

[3] *Euthanasia and the Right to Death*, ed. A. B. Downing, Peter Owen, (1969), page 103.
[4] *A Plan for Voluntary Euthanasia* (1962), page 18. Our italics.
[5] *Ibid.*, page 20. Original italics.

Assembly of the United Nations.'[6] However, no new legal right is required to achieve this. The right to a dignified and merciful death has the approval of the law and of all the churches. The non-statutory declaration suggested by Miss Barrington in the same book declining 'any treatment or sustenance designed to prolong my life'[7] is framed in too wide terms, as treatment and sustenance in a conscious patient may sometimes provide relief of suffering as well as prolonging life.

What the various efforts to introduce euthanasia legislation have aimed at has been the legalisation not of the right to die— a palpable absurdity—but of the right to kill. This, even with the patient's consent and at his request (anyway supposedly so) is a very different matter. 'The *direct* ending of a life, with or without the patient's consent, is euthanasia in its simple, unsophisticated and ethically candid form' writes J. Fletcher.[8] His further sentence in this connection : 'A decision *not* to keep a patient alive is as morally deliberate as a decision to *end* life'[9] strikes strange. Of course a decision to do a wise or good act is as deliberate as a decision to do a foolish or wicked act, but that does not make the two acts morally equal. The reader of that sentence might be forgiven for inferring that in its author's opinion, because the two decisions are equally deliberate, they are either equally culpable or equally praiseworthy, which clearly they are not. The same remark will strike doubly strange to the reader who pursues his study of that book into the next chapter, for there he will find George P. Fletcher emphasising strongly the distinction between causing harm and permitting harm to occur.

To relieve pain and distress remains the doctor's first task, and he has plenty of means to help him, whether the patient's suffering is physical or mental. The medical conquest of distress is still not complete, but even so the Euthanasia Society has this to say about hospitals for terminal illnesses : 'Most of these hospitals are staffed by dedicated women belonging to some religious order, many of whom are also trained in nursing. Experience has shown

[6] *Euthanasia and the Right to Death*, page 5.
[7] *Ibid.*, page 171.   [8] *Ibid.*, page 68. Original italics.
[9] *Ibid.*, loc. cit. Original italics.

that in the sympathetic and sometimes surprisingly cheerful atmosphere created by these women . . . they (the patients) are able to face death when it comes with a quiet mind—unafraid. Even if euthanasia were permissible to these patients probably very few would wish to avail themselves of it.'[10]

The authors of the pamphlet say that these circumstances are exceptional, because there are few such terminal hospitals, and this fact is used as support for the legalisation of euthanasia. What an indictment against our society, to propose killing people because there is not enough sympathy for them! If the old are a burden on their relations, the solution is to make proper provision for them. This was pointed out by several speakers in the Debate in the House of Lords on the Voluntary Euthanasia Bill 1969.

In those cases where a patient 'merely exists', it is not he who suffers but those around him. In the words of the Euthanasia Society's spokesman: 'Dying is still often an ugly business',[11] but where should we end up once we admitted the principle that a man may be killed for the benefit of someone else?

Medical judgement is fallible and, with ever-increasing medical skill, conditions may be curable tomorrow that are incurable today. To this argument the Euthanasia Society retorts that 'the remote possibility of making a mistake is not a reason for doing nothing'.[12] The safeguard mentioned in that context is—or at least in the 1962 pamphlet was—'that patients will seldom seriously consider the termination of life before such gross damage has been done to vital organs that recovery is out of the question';[13] but this point has lost its validity since a declaration in advance was incorporated into the Euthanasia Society's proposals.

Once a patient has signed a declaration, possibly even before he has signed it but when he knows the family expects him to do so, pride or a false sense of duty may prevent him, despite his distress, from changing his decision even though he has changed his mind. Such change of mind may be due only to a natural fear

---

[10] *A Plan for Voluntary Euthanasia* (1962), page 19.
[11] *Ibid.*, page 6.   [12] *Ibid.*, page 24.   [13] *Ibid., loc. cit.*

of death now the patient actually has to face it, but it may equally well be due to an experience of conversion or recovery of faith. There are certainly many instances known of this, so that clearly the spiritual state of a patient must not be assumed to remain static during a terminal illness. Moreover, where the patient's mind is clouded but still receptive, or his expression is impaired, how could an independent assessing doctor become aware, or be made aware, of a change of mind? The ethical point at issue here is that in the circumstances the doctor has no access to information from the patient on which he can conscientiously base a decision which is both professionally and ethically sound.

A patient might be suffering from an incurable disease but still be capable of leading a gratifying life for a long time; who would decide, and by what criteria, when he was to be liquidated? For cases like carcinoma of the throat with difficulty in swallowing and breathing, the Euthanasia Society argues that, though few express it, 'we cannot know how many have harboured that wish (for release) secretly'.[14] To this, it must be answered that we do not know either how many fear the end, and might fear it more if they had signed declarations and wondered at what stage their 'Will' might be executed.

Supporters of euthanasia urge that the quality of life is more important than the quantity. This slogan misleads many people: what is meant by quality? What criteria can be used to judge it, and by what possible standards can anybody assess the level of quality below which life is worthless?

Lord Ailwyn argued in the debate on Lord Raglan's Bill that those who believe in an after-life should agree that a suffering mortal be given the right to be wafted painlessly into it. Followed to its logical conclusion this would lead to the obviously absurd inference that Christian babies should be killed as soon as they are baptised, as that would guarantee their going straight to heaven.

The opposition to the legalisation of euthanasia stems from the realisation that permissive legislation would end in the encouragement of what is, in fact, in Lord Cork and Orrery's phrase,

[14] *Ibid.*, page 21.

'suicide by proxy'. Of course there are some who not only defend but extol suicide and consider the 'indoctrination' against it to be regrettable.[15] The law of the land no longer allows prosecution for attempted suicide, but in abstaining from prosecution it does not express approval : in practice it treats attempted suicide as evidence of mental disturbance. Suicide pacts, and any encouragement to or help with a suicide, are still offences in law. Flew, in his essay on 'The Principle of Euthanasia', states that he is concerned primarily with general principles and is not discussing— except perhaps quite incidentally—'any questions of comparative detail'.[16] Such a position is untenable : these general principles cannot be separated from practicalities. Whenever risk of error or abuse exists, as it certainly would in the practice of euthanasia, the question must be asked, 'How compelling is the need to implement the principle?'—particularly so when the soundness of the principle is itself in doubt.

The supporters of euthanasia consider that the doctor-patient relationship would not be damaged if euthanasia were available. In *A Plan for Voluntary Euthanasia* (1962) this was one of the 'Arguments commonly employed against euthanasia' which the authors sought to refute (page 18 et seq). On page 24 they state :

(12)   The legalisation of euthanasia would tend to undermine the confidence of patients in their doctors, and would even lead some patients to fear that euthanasia might be used without their consent.

Comment

On the contrary, the safeguards in the proposed Bill should help to allay such fears. And many people approaching old age would certainly find comfort in the assurance that their doctor would be sympathetic to their request for relief if a terminal illness should bring unbearable suffering. Medical men are not infrequently asked to give such an assurance.

Scrutiny of this statement shows that use of the term 'relief' is ambiguous and perhaps euphemistic. If 'relief of suffering' only

[15] *Euthanasia and the Right to Death,* page 153.
[16] *Ibid.,* page 31.

is meant, then the proponents of euthanasia are asking no more than is common, decent medical practice. If, however, 'relief' means the deliberate and intentional ending of life, why do they not say so, for this is an entirely different matter? Why obscure the difference?

The patient trusts his doctor to care for him to the best of his ability. However hard-pressed a family doctor may be, he will find time for a confidential talk with his dying patient. Knowing the family background, he will more quickly arrive at sound conclusions than another doctor, and his encouragement and comfort will be more easily accepted by his patient. But if the doctor had undertaken to observe his patient's requests (see the schedule to the 1969 Bill (p. 143), which empowers the patient to specify the time or indicate the circumstances of his death), even though the doctor had grounds for regarding these requests as no longer relevant or applicable, then the doctor would be in a position where he could no longer freely serve the best interests of his patient. This is an example of the type of damage that could be done to the doctor-patient relationship from the doctor's point of view : the implications could be far-reaching.

There might be tensions anyway in the home of an incurably ill man, but there is a great difference between those which the healthy relatives may have to bear in struggling with their mixed emotions, and the tensions which might arise between the patient and those surrounding him through a petition for euthanasia, or perhaps more often by a failure to petition. Particularly, children of vulnerable age would suffer from the effects of the discussions that would necessarily go on in a family before such a decision was made, and which it would be impossible to conceal from them. Obviously, so long as there is no provision in law for a petition for death, forecasts of what might happen if there were must be speculative. Nevertheless, such speculation can be fairly based on clinical observation, and such observation shows that there is more concern on the part of relatives that a patient should not be allowed to linger on in 'unnecessary suffering' than there is on the part of the patient himself.

Underlying the whole controversy is a difference of approach to the value of human life. On the one hand the tradition, not only of Christendom but of all civilised people, gives to human life a respect above that accorded to animal life, and of a different sort: on the other hand there are those who dismiss this respect as misplaced. Thus J. R. Wilson writes: 'We are all supposed to feel some deep inherent reverence for human life',[17] the implication being not only that some people do not feel such reverence, but also that there is at least an element of superstition in such feeling. To accept that line of thought is to reduce men to the stature of animals—a notion offensive to common sense. 'People take the experience of killing very easily inded; it is the disapproval of society which bothers them', the same author adds. Taken together with the preceding thought, it seems that Wilson considers it enlightened to feel free to kill, and old-fashioned to disapprove of killing. These quotations illustrate the type of thinking which underlies the case for euthanasia.

However closely and carefully an Act might be framed in order to ensure that euthanasia was committed only in certain strictly defined circumstances, those circumstances would in practice be read into every conceivable case by those who wished to practice euthanasia, while those who declined could be denounced as failing to implement the law of the land, or to give patients 'their rights'.

Though no forecast concerning the long-term consequences of a Voluntary Euthanasia Act can be infallible, the suspicion that the voluntary aspect of it would not last long is certainly not to be dismissed as scaremongering. Lord Chorley gave a pointer in this direction during the 1950 Debate in the House of Lords: 'Another objection is that the Bill does not go far enough . . . that may be so, but we *must go step by step*.'[18] More recently, the Earl of Listowel, though pleading for voluntary euthanasia only, added the ominous words '. . . we cannot wish to preserve an anonymous individual who has been stripped of personality and reduced by incessant pain or physical deterioration to the animal

---

[17] J. R. Wilson, 'The Freedom to Die', *The Spectator*, 7 February 1969.
[18] Hansard, H. of L., vol 169, col 559. Our italics.

or vegetable level'.[19] Lord Listowel is here putting forward a highly coloured picture of a rare case, but is putting it forward as if it were commonplace. Moreover, as should be clear from what has been said earlier, the perpetuation of a merely breathing body is not currently good medical practice.

Once the principle of the sanctity of human life is abandoned, or the propaganda accepted that to uphold it is old-fashioned, prejudiced or superstitious, the way is open to the raising of—and the satisfaction of—a demand for so-called euthanasia for severely handicapped children, the mentally sub-normal, the severely crippled, the aged, and ultimately for all who are a burden on the community services and the public purse.

Medicine—and thus its practitioner—is essentially concerned with the relief of pain and suffering and the furtherance of the well-being of the individual.[20] For this reason, whenever the doctor is involved (and he is necessarily involved in this matter) his approach must be an individual one. Nevertheless there is no antithesis between the ultimate good of the individual and that of society. To those who believe in the brotherhood of man, whether from religious or humanist considerations, such an antithesis must appear as a contradiction in terms.

The small families of the 1920's and 30's have left us in the 1960's and 70's with a high proportion of elderly people. Euthanasia could make the sick elderly a ready target for an unwholesome social policy—indeed their destruction might improve the appearance of the population statistics. Let euthanasia be seen for what it is : a tragic attempt to patch up a morbid society.

[19] *Euthanasia and the Right to Death*, page 6.
[20] J. Gould, 'The Psychiatry of Major Crime', *Recent Progress in Psychiatry*, vol III (1958).

Chapter VII

The care of the incurable and the dying

This story is recounted under the title 'The treatment of a case of incurable disease' in the *British Medical Journal* 1968 :[1] a sixty-eight year old doctor, who five years earlier had had a coronary thrombosis, was discovered to have a large carcinoma of the stomach. Operation showed that the growth had spread to involve the liver and the glands of the abdomen. The actual growth itself was removed to prevent perforation of the tumour and to relieve the pain produced. There was evidence of spread of the growth to the spine when this was x-rayed. However, the patient remained in severe pain, needing large doses of pain relieving drugs. On the tenth day after the operation he collapsed with a large blood clot on the lung. This was successfully removed by an emergency operation. Two weeks later his heart stopped due to a coronary thrombosis; he was revived by the hospital's emergency resuscitation team. That night his heart stopped four more times and each time was restarted artificially. For three weeks the patient lingered on unconscious, maintained by intravenous feeding, blood transfusions and antibiotics. Arrangements were being made to put him on a mechanical artificial respirator when the heart finally stopped.

It can be fairly said that in this case the measures of resuscitation applied, including the removal of the blood clot in the lung artery, were largely useless. The patient was in severe pain; he

[1] W. St C. Symmers Sen., *British Medical Journal* (1968) 1, 442 (17 February, correspondence).

had very little time to live and the measures taken could in no way cure or improve the underlying cancer.

A doctor should avoid carrying out treatment for its own sake, or for the sake of devotion to professional expertise, when it is clear that the treatment is going to be virtually useless.

The amount of discomfort and suffering that a person can bear and the amount of sheer effort that a person can put into the task of sustaining life and health is always limited but very variable from one person to another. It may be useful to consider the extent of a man's duty in this regard and to relate this to the practical care of incurable and dying people.

Broadly speaking one can classify the means of maintaining life and health into three main groups. The first consists of every-day measures such as taking of food and drink in adequate amounts. The second consists of usual, commonly used, medical methods of treatment. The third consists of those methods of treatment which are described as 'extraordinary'. The second group—usual, commonly used medical treatment—comprises those methods which are effective, involve little risk to life and which do not cause a disproportionate amount of pain or other distress or difficulty to the patient. Treatment by medicines, pills, injections, intravenous infusions and blood transfusions and the routinely used, highly effective, low risk operations, such as re-moval of the appendix, or gall bladder or the setting of a broken limb, come into this category. Other examples are external cardiac massage and artificial respiration used for short periods of time. The third group, extraordinary methods, involves more risk, pain and distress to the patient and the benefit, though it may be great, is less predictable. Examples of such treatment are transplanta-tion of whole organs such as kidney or heart, and prolonged artificial respiration for an unconscious patient.

Those who accept the general principle that a person has a duty to sustain his own health and life would nonetheless agree that no one has any moral obligation to undergo treatment by 'extraordinary' means. They would also agree that every patient has the right to refuse any form of treatment that may be offered to him.

In the case of a frail elderly patient or a sick person suffering several illnesses at the same time, treatment which would otherwise be accepted as usual could become extraordinary. In these types of cases the efficacy of a given treatment would be reduced by virtue of the patient's state; the risk would be increased and the possibility that the patient would be severely distressed by treatment would become much greater. Thus, intravenous feeding, or even a course of antibiotics given by injection might become 'extraordinary' remedies for a particular patient. .

The doctor who is going to prescribe treatment that may be distressing or risky always obtains, if possible, the explicit or implicit permission of the patient before carrying it out. It is normal to have written permission for a surgical operation, when the patient is capable of giving it. If the patient is too ill to give permission, a doctor will normally use all such methods as are available to maintain life as long as there is a reasonable chance of cure or significant improvement in the patient's condition. When this is no longer so, he limits himself to forms of treatment which do not cause distress, and to relief of symptoms such as pain, restlessness and vomiting.

In the case of the unconscious patient being maintained alive by intravenous feeding and artificial respiration, the doctor need not persist indefinitely with treatment if he judges that recovery of consciousness is impossible. If special equipment, for instance a respirator, is being used in the treatment of such a hopeless case and is needed for another patient who has a good chance of recovery, then the latter has the better claim to the equipment.

The nurse-doctor team caring for the patient with incurable disease seeks his good and his happiness by kindness and compassion, accepting him as a person and not just as a disease entity, and trying to understand his sufferings, fears, frustrations and moods. Thus small discomforts should be relieved as much as possible; here nurses have the major part to play when the patient is in hospital; at home they share this role with the patient's relatives.

The distinction in principle between the incidental shortening of life by giving a drug for the purpose of relieving pain and the identical relief of pain by giving a drug to cause death has been drawn elsewhere in this book. From the practical point of view the difference between these two courses is striking; in the first case the doctor estimates the dose of the drug and frequency of administration which will relieve distress and pain; in the other case he would have to estimate the dose that would kill. Usually pain relieving and tranquillizing drugs are given together when pain is due to terminal cancer, so that there is some persistent drowsiness which will dull apprehension. There is no reason why the moribund patient should not be kept in a state of unconsciousness should he so desire. But some prefer to remain more awake and alert, in which case pain can still be greatly relieved by suitable drugs. In the case of the patient who wishes to be rendered continuously unconscious prior to death, it would be proper to ensure that he has had an opportunity, which he has recognised at such, to put his affairs in order. For some this would mean no more than material affairs, for others it may include personal and spiritual matters including receiving the sacraments.

However, pain is not the inevitable accompaniment of terminal disease. Dr Exton-Smith[2] has given an account of 220 patients, all over sixty, dying from various diseases. Only thirty of these had moderate or severe pain during their terminal illness and a further seventeen complained of other distressing symptoms such as vomiting or shortness of breath. Of these 220 patients, thirty-three had cancer. Over half the cancer patients had no pain at all; about a quarter had pain that could be relieved by simple pain relieving drugs such as aspirin, while rather less than a quarter experienced moderate or severe pain which could be relieved by morphine-type drugs. The average duration of the painful terminal stage of the illness in this last group was six and a half weeks.

Of the whole 220 patients, about forty per cent were persistently confused and unaware of the extent of their disabilities and their progressive decline.

Depressive illness may occur in a patient with incurable disease. Even when a patient is in the last few months of life the depression

[2] A. N. Exton-Smith, *The Lancet* (1961) 2, 305.

may prove readily responsive to treatment by current very effective drugs which are anti-depressant. Such favourable responses can occur even in those whose cancer has already spread widely and who prove to have only six or nine months to live, as well as in others suffering persistent crippling illness such as widespread arthritis or the after-effects of a stroke. Untreated depression in the incurable sick may be associated with suicidal desires just as occurs in depression in any other setting and can lead to an expressed wish for death.

In patients who are fit enough to have it, electro-convulsive therapy may work if drugs fail, though this would be used in terminal cancer only with circumspection.

Certain special situations in the care of the incurable may now be considered. Deterioration of mental powers in varying degrees is very common in the elderly, leading to persistent or fluctuating confusion and forgetfulness. No one cares to look forward to this state, which may be combined with physical incapacity and incontinence. Nevertheless, one should not exaggerate the suffering of the elderly patient who is becoming demented. He is usually contented when he is well cared for in pleasant surroundings with adequate facilities for nursing. He lives for the moment, not conscious of disabilities. His wants and desires are gradually reduced to the basic ones—food, drink, physical comfort, and friendliness and patience on the part of those caring for him. Such a patient may not be prepossessing, but he appreciates kindness even when deterioration is quite advanced and he is bedfast. Affectionate attachment to the patients characterises many if not most who work in geriatric homes or wards.

The very nature of the conditions described limits the doctor's freedom and scope in treating any further supervening illness, for treatment readily becomes distressing to the patient. Within the clinical scope available, which varies from case to case and in the same case from time to time, the aim of care will be to relieve conditions which are curable. Treatment which serves but to prolong the process of dying would be avoided. As illustrations of these principles, the use of various techniques may be considered. Antibiotics in pneumonia could be curative in one case and merely distressing, delaying death in another. Intravenous feeding may save the life of one but prolong distressfully the death of another. Feeding by stomach tube might help one and unprofitably upset another. In each case the judgement rests upon the physician and must be formed for each patient at a given time.

When one is treating elderly patients it is very difficult to foresee the outcome of treatment whether as to death or degree of social recovery.[3] Because of this, in a ward of long stay patients the aim is to maintain an atmosphere of active treatment. This includes physiotherapy, diversion and recreation. Pleasant surroundings too are most helpful. Then the patients know that they are being cared for and not merely tolerated as they suffer and deteriorate. Companionship is important; visiting by friends and relatives matters and so should be encouraged; and visiting hours should be as elastic as possible.

Patients do sometimes ask to be given something to 'put me to sleep'. This request (which may be due to normal anxiety) is usually made in a state of depression during recovery from an acute or subacute episode of illness when improvement is slow, the degree of recovery unsure, and when there are uncertainties about the future care of the patient. The request to be put to sleep is one of the opportunities a doctor can take to talk to the patient and show that personal interest which may remove the fear of being a burden that in part led to the request in the first place. One of the greatest needs both of the dying and of the incurable is knowledge that they are being looked after willingly. In hospital, nurses play the greater part in removing the fear of being a burden, but all grades of staff are involved, including porters and domestics.

At home, relatives, with the district nurse, carry the load of looking after a sick person. Most long term illness is looked after at home, where more than half of all deaths occur.

It often happens that those who see patients, whether young or old, suffering severe physical deformity, emaciation or mental deterioration, experience horror and repugnance. The natural

[3] D. W. K. Kay et al., 'Psychiatric Disorders of the Elderly', *Journal of the Mental Sciences* (1956) January, 129.

desire to be rid of such ugliness can lead to the desire for the death of the so afflicted. The feeling of horror and repugnance may well be challenged in the individual onlooker by feelings of sympathy and pity. He may well interpret his desire for the death of the individual as the outcome of these more tender feelings, so that he may, with peaceful conscience, nonetheless express his need to be rid of an unpleasant spectacle. This desire in the observer may be quite unrelated to any actual suffering the patient is undergoing. For instance, a patient in prolonged coma is not suffering at all. Doctors and nurses are not immune to this reaction, and it is one which they have consciously to control so that they can care for such people with kindness and friendliness.

If doctors and nurses were ever to come to accept that killing patients was an acceptable way of 'treating' disease and suffering, they would inevitably at times and in regard to particular patients feel that such patients ought to ask for euthanasia. This would colour their attitudes towards such patients and might well lead the patients to feel rejected and unwanted. This would be an unspoken pressure on them to ask for euthanasia, for it would lessen the friendliness of the staff and their care for details of their patients' comfort, which are the main safeguards against the patients' sense of being a burden. They would become more anxious and fearful or resentful, and might eventually ask for death. For the staff concerned, the killing could then seem to be only the removal of an unwanted burden; but in fact it would be a final rejection of one of their fellow men.

The book *Sans Everything*[4] shows what may happen if callousness develops among hospital staff and it also shows very vividly the effects of inadequate numbers of staff working under unsatisfactory conditions, with overcrowded wards, inadequate facilities and in unpleasant surroundings. This underlines the fact that it is difficult to get the community to spend money on intermediate and long stay wards of all types. Is society going to be tempted to solve this problem by imposing on doctors and nurses the duty of killing patients who ask to be killed and by providing only the

[4] B. Robb, *Sans Everything, a Case to Answer* (London, 1967).

type of long stay hospitals which will encourage people to ask for death?

Finally, what of the feelings of patients in a ward where one of them has just been killed? In elderly patients one occasionally sees a condition of pathological suspicion of nursing and medical staff, when the individual refuses treatment because he thinks he is being poisoned. Would not this kind of reaction be more likely to occur if 'therapeutic killing' became part of the accepted conduct of doctors and nurses? This is considered in more detail in the next chapter.

Chapter VIII

The human problems of euthanasia

So far the argument has been pursued on grounds of general considerations almost to the exclusion of the personal problem. The
proponents of euthanasia frequently make their appeals on general
grounds, and then quote or cite individual cases illustrating their
points as if such cases proved the validity of the argument put
forward.[1] In this chapter the person as distinct from the principle
is considered, and we examine the human problems which could
and would have arisen had the 1969 Voluntary Euthanasia Bill,
or indeed any imaginable Bill legalising euthanasia, become law
in this country.

Pain and suffering are inescapable at times in life, and sometimes attend its end. To relieve such pain and suffering is the aim
of those who promote euthanasia; it is no less the aim of those
who, like the writers of this book, oppose euthanasia as it is put
forward to Parliament. Pain, it is to be remembered, is a natural
response of the human body to many damaging or injurious
incidents or experiences. It is an alerting signal promoting avoid-
ance or retaliation in the simple case of pain of external origin.
Generally pain can be considered natural and wholesome although
unpleasant. Pain is difficult to assess as to degree or intensity and
many individual and cultural factors enter into the mode of its

---

[1] See, for example the speeches of Lord Archibald and Lord Ritchie-
Calder, in the 1969 debate referred to on pp. 59–60 or that of Lord Chorley
in the 1950 debate (p. 45). See also *Euthanasia and the Right to Death*,
page 17 and elsewhere.

endurance and the way it is regarded both by sufferer and by observer.[2]

Pain arising from disease is in many ways more obscure. In our present age much can be done to alleviate it; but this has not always been so, and in the farther past the resources of medicine were poorer as far as cure of the disease or morbid condition was concerned. Whereas in the past the endurance of pain was accepted as a part of living and of illness and it was therefore laudable to exhibit fortitude, now, when pain can be so much more readily relieved, there is more apparent a vociferous if minority opinion favouring the complete abolition of pain. While we are not supporting the endurance of pain for its own sake, the idea that all pain is necessarily to be abolished is unsound. Had we been organisms incapable of experiencing pain, our capacity for survival would have been and would be reduced.

The legalisation of medical killing of sick persons would create far more distress, suffering and pain, directly and indirectly, than it would relieve. The human grounds on which this statement rests are given in this and the next chapter. One cannot separate neatly and clearly each from the other, the patient, his relatives, his nurses and doctors, and his fellow patients. These, and society as a whole, are all interconnected and the repercussions of medical killing would pervade all of them. Furthermore the provisions of the 1969 Bill would have required not only the collaboration of doctors and nurses but also, as witnesses to the required declaration, the participation of other ordinary men and women.

It is implicit in the literature of the Euthanasia Society and in the Bills for Euthanasia that doctors and nurses would be prepared to collaborate in the deliberate termination of the life of the patient who wishes to be killed. But would they? So far there has been no adequate investigation of the attitudes of doctors and nurses to the suggestion that they be made the ministers of death, although a very limited enquiry is described below in Chapter X. The authors of *A Plan for Voluntary Euthanasia* expect a small

[2] For a fuller discussion on this, see J. Gould, 'The Assessment of Pain in Clinical Practice', *British Journal of Clinical Practice*, vol 16, no 1 (January 1962).

number of 'qualified patients' in the first instance so that only a small number of doctors and nurses would, initially, need to be prepared to implement the Act, provided they and the qualified patients could be brought together.[3] The practice could then be expected to grow, presumably because killing by medical means can be swift, painless, noiseless and bloodless. Were doctors ready to implement the act not geographically available to the qualified patients there could well arise the cry that the sick were being 'denied their right'. In fact duly registered medical practitioners and officially qualified nurses are not even essential to the act of killing the qualified patient.

The 1968 Draft Bill was adopted in principle at the 1967 Annual General Meeting of the Euthanasia Society. Supporting it at the meeting Miss Mary Rose Barrington said (and her address was circulated as an appendix to the minutes of that meeting): 'We are up against the difficulty that so far as the medical profession is concerned the Bill is purely permissive, and not mandatory.' In other words if she had her way, the doctor would be compelled by law to implement euthanasia. She continued, 'It would be very easy to draft so as to please only the bold and resolute, but we feel it behoves us to be a little more complicated so as to cater also for the wavering and timorous.'

Miss Barrington's underlying assumptions seem to be:

(i) That doctors and nurses—professions notoriously difficult to organise in some ways—will regard what is made legal as being thereby made morally or ethically justified, and in due course will come to regard what is made legal as virtually compulsory.

(ii) The introduction of Voluntary Euthanasia for certain sick people will serve as a means of introducing euthanasia as a social phenomenon, to be applied also to the 'timorous and wavering' patient. Euthanasia here means, let it be remembered, the deliber-

---

[3] The proponents state (page 9): 'On that assumption such an Act would bring relief to some 900-1,000 cancer cases a year in England and Wales—perhaps considerably more. With the sufferers from other diseases the total might well add up to 3,000 or 4,000 and increase as the years go by.' These estimates must be seen in the setting of the annual death rate which is approximately 600,000; the estimate is thus 0.5% of deaths.

ate killing of one person by another, the latter being legally authorised to do so.

It is proper to consider some of the implications of a doctor being authorised to kill an appropriately sick and duly assenting person. If the doctor, being not kith or kin, have the right so to kill, what then of the blood tie? Have not the relatives a similar right? What of the parents with the child suffering from 'an irremediable condition' especially if no doctor ready to administer euthanasia (i.e. kill the child) be available, or even readily available? By the same token, what of the aged parent suffering an 'irremediable condition' where no application for euthanasia has been officially prepared but a doctor is put under pressure to act with humanity in the best interests of mercy for the patient (and the relatives)? Could not the relatives 'in conscience and mercy' feel free to kill in such circumstances? Once the doctors really become as George Bernard Shaw described them, 'the licenced killers', how should the good and merciful intentions of the family be stemmed? And where then is the dividing line to be drawn?

Try now to conceive of the practical issues involved in the nursing and medical care of the 'qualified patient'.

(a)   In his own home (where one half of all deaths occur).
(b)   In a single room in a hospital or nursing home.
(c)   In a ward of a hospital.

In these situations the patient is surrounded by relatives, nurses and doctors. In the hospital ward, other patients also are involved. These last may or may not be 'qualified' patients and their appreciation of the legal protection conferred upon them by *not* having signed certificates for euthanasia may be very vague, for once admitted to hospital, a person's sense of independence is to some extent reduced as he must submit to the hospital regime. Increase of dependency occurs too in one's own home or the home of one's children once chronic illness reduces the freedom to do things for oneself. With increasing dependency due to sickness in any setting one's sense of one's rights becomes impaired. It is to be remembered that what is here discussed is not the easement of the pathway to death permitting life to come to its end with as little mental or physical distress as possible, for this is current practice and rightly so. What is here discussed is the outright killing of one who, as far as present legislative proposals are concerned, is suffering from an 'irremediable condition'.

The Patient in His Own Home[4]

He is in his own home; he is 'qualified' and certified for killing (euthanasia) and the necessary thirty days have passed since the signing of the declaration. Imagine the uncertainty on the part of the patient at the entry of the doctor or nurse—to be killed now or to be made, by *not* being killed, to live another hour or another day? Or will he be given some pill or injection to induce the final sleep in which his life will be ended? Desdemona, it is true, was not a candidate for voluntary euthanasia, but her plea to Othello, 'Kill me tomorrow, my Lord, Let me live this night' might well become a commonplace remark.[5]

Shall the patient to be killed be segregated from the members of his family, or shall he be attended by them to be supported by their affection? Shall they be present at the fatal ministration or only before and after? Should the patient or the members of the family know at which precise moment the ministry of death is to be applied? Or should all be in ignorance? And if all are to

---

[4] The 1969 Bill is couched in some parts in phrases which seem to imply that euthanasia would always be administered under the Bill in hospital, but on scrutiny the Bill does not preclude the administration of euthanasia in the patient's own home. It could well be expected that at some stage in the passage of the Bill legalising euthanasia there would be written into it a clause specially providing for home administration of euthanasia. Without such explicit provision, there would be justifiable resentment that qualified patients were obliged to go to hospital or to a nursing home to be killed instead of enjoying death administered in the privacy of their own homes.

[5] Many have faced their known time of death or killing by the headsman, the hangman, the firing squad, and other means held appropriate to society. There is little in these experiences to indicate that ordinary people so marked out were complacent. While capital punishment continued to be practised is this country, prisoners well away from the gaol concerned were noticeably subdued on the hanging day. No ordinary man or woman wishes to be snuffed out. The idea of instant death in this age of instant medicine and instant many things may have its appeal while it is purely speculative and in the folds of the future; it is less appealing as it comes closer, unless, some feel, death should snatch us unexpectedly when we are not awaiting the event.

be in ignorance, save the doctor or the hapless nurse, what will be the effect on the patient and the relatives as the doctor or nurse comes into the room to kill? Is it to be supposed that the doctor or nurse will betray no evidence of the fact that it has been decided in his or her mind that the patient's 'time has come'? It could be that among those of us reared in the healing tradition of medicine there may be some who secretly find gratification in suffering or even in the infliction of death. But if the secret gratification no longer had to be kept secret, because killing patients under certain conditions had become lawful, we might expect the killer-doctor or killer-nurse to betray some small sign of his enjoyment. If so, what of this in regard to the patient and the relatives? And what of the subsequent reactions of the relatives? Would one of the doctors who had helped prepare the certificates qualifying the patient for killing be the family doctor? And will he be the one to whom the relatives turn for help later if they grieve or suffer regret or remorse? With what conviction could that doctor comfort or reassure the relatives afterwards? How, in fact, could the relatives accept such help from that doctor or indeed from any member of the medical profession in their plight? Normal grief comprises in its course one phase when the mourner reflects on his real or imagined defects in the care of and attention to the departed. In the presence of long drawn out terminal illness such mourning may go on, piecemeal as it were, before the death of the invalid. So also, concurrently, there occur resentment and fatigue (in the sense of coming to the end of one's tether) in caring for, or even visiting, the slowly dying patient.

In the case of a patient legally killed by euthanasia it could of course rationally be urged that the patient had made his own declaration and was duly 'qualified' and lawfully exterminated. But this is too facile an argument, for humans are not merely rational. They are much more than that. They feel; and although many feelings go beyond rationality, while remaining socially acceptable and comprehensible to other people, they are far from irrational. Rationality is a form of thinking which proceeds under two principles, (i) reason, (ii) expedient relation to external reality in order to preserve or promote one's comfort and/or well-being, in the longer or shorter term. Thus even rationality comprises a modicum of feeling. But in proportion as feelings become stronger so rational considerations are less likely to hold sway. The occasions of the critical events in life, particularly birth, accidents, severe illness and bereavement, are more liable to provoke strong feeling. When death occurs, mourning follows. Mourning gone bad, or pathological mourning, to put it more technically, may well become depression in its medical sense, with attendant impairment of drive, initiative, interest, energy and pleasure in living. Where mourning is mixed with significant guilt and anxiety, depression is more likely to supervene, and with depression (in the medical sense) there is the well-known attendant implication, or implicit threat, of suicide.

Are we to assume that the existence of a statute will alter the mental constitution of man? Perhaps life would be more simple if this were so. Or are we to take note that a statute has been twice proposed which relies in too facile and narrow a fashion upon the rational components of man's mind and disregards the more personal reactions of those involved in actions and assents which run directly counter to the values of our society hitherto?

Having considered the qualified patient in his own home among his relatives and the implications of the legalised killing of him in some detail, the consideration of the other groups may be briefer.

The Patient in a Single Room in Hospital or Nursing Home

He is in similar case to the patient in his own home but for one factor. The hospital or nursing home is less homely, more impersonal and the administration lends to this quality. The patient becomes more acquiescent and dependent. The relatives may feel that much, if not all, of the responsibility has been lifted from them and accepted by the medical and nursing staff, as commonly occurs when a patient is admitted to a hospital ward.

The Patient in the Hospital Ward

The patient suffering a condition which he comes privately to believe, while still clear in mind, may be irremediable or incurable, may rationally appreciate that his life is not legally in jeopardy. Remove him to a more impersonal situation such as a hospital and, especially if aged, his sense of security in nurses and doctors could readily be undermined, as he watches events in the ward and sees that another patient has died. How will he interpret this, once he knows that killing has been made lawful? Are patients in wards to be told which patients have died naturally and which have been legally exterminated?

Anxiety in the patient admitted to hospital has recently been so well recognised that various procedures have become widespread in an attempt to assuage it. These include booklets about the hospital, and its administration; the procedure for admission; what services are available such as social workers and how visiting may be arranged. These booklets are issued to patients prior to admission and hospitals have also sought to make the admission procedure more informal. To the same end there has been an increase in visiting hours thus permitting more frequent visits by relatives and friends.

Old people and unsophisticated people readily become apprehensive if their trust in the hospital be undermined. However circumscribed an Act of Parliament may be to the lawyer, the existence of a legal right to kill a sick person will not be reassuring to the many who, in protracted illness requiring hospital care, come to feel a burden to themselves and others, while they are yet ambivalent about living if not still actively clinging to life.

Some readers will remember the fear of emotionally sick people of 'being put away' prior to the introduction of modern reforms of the Acts relating to mental illness. The proponents of euthanasia could well, were they to succeed in getting an Act on to the Statute Book, set stalking a bigger ogre than was laid by the 1934 Act which permitted voluntary treatment in mental hospitals and by the Mental Health Act 1959 which rendered such treatment quite informal. How would the doctors and nurses be able to reassure the anxious invalid? Could he trust the doctor or nurse not to kill him when he fears that the nurse or doctor killed the patient in the next bed? What good to explain to an old, unsophisticated and very sick man the niceties of 'voluntary' as opposed to 'mere' euthanasia! He will not comprehend: all he will 'know' is, 'They're allowed to kill us nowadays.'

As an alternative to the administration of euthanasia to a qualified patient in a ward, with the likelihood of spreading rumour and anxiety, one could envisage the removal of the patient to a special room for the legal termination of his life. If some of the ward nurses escorted him out of the ward and they, but not he, returned, are we in much better case than we were before? How would the remaining patients view the returning nurses? What would they make of any transfer from the ward whether it was said to be for different treatment or for any other reason? Would the doctors or nurses administering euthanasia be known to be doing so? How would other patients, chronically ill, care to be attended by them? Or will there be a special caste of doctors and nurses who devote themselves, peripatetically, to the killing, their colleagues having completed the certificates?

Human Problems and Administration

Will the patient be admitted to a hospital specially designated for and perhaps even reserved for euthanasia? And will such hospitals be known for what they are? If hospitals are to be used, shall private wings of hospitals be used? Shall private nursing homes be used? Shall they advertise their activities, in print or by word of mouth? And how will the patient and his relatives and others not yet due to enter, look upon these establishments and the members of their staff?

How shall the ministers of death and all the ancillary staff, domestics, porters, mortuary attendants (as well as nurses and doctors) be paid? Or shall they be asked to do this work as a voluntary, compassionate service? If they are to be paid for their services, shall these services be regarded as part and parcel of their work under the National Health Service—that itself was called into being in part in consequence of Lord Beveridge's call for the conquest of the three giants, Want, Squalor and Disease? It would indeed be ironical if the conquest of disease were achieved by killing the sick and suffering person so that the disease had no longer a matrix or setting in which to persist! If the staff are not to be paid for killing as part of their services under the National Health Service shall they receive special remuneration from other sources for their participation in implementing the legislation on euthanasia? Who then will negotiate, or decide the death-administration fee? What standards will be involved in setting the fee and in its alteration?

It is part of the established system of our society that, although all contribute by taxes and in other ways to the costs of the National Health Service, any citizen is free to make private arrangements for his medical care. We are used to making our personal and private arrangements, also, for our funerals. What then of our personal and private arrangements for our death? Is it easily to be envisaged that we arrange a private death-accommodation fee for the private room in a hospital, and privately arrange with our family doctor and the consultants and nurses their remuneration for killing us?

Chapter IX

What the 1969 Bill could have meant in practice

The 1969 Voluntary Euthanasia Bill has been scrutinised from a legal point of view in Chapters III and V. Here it is proposed to examine its principal clauses in relation to the patients, doctors and nurses who would have been involved had it become law. It is to be remembered that this Bill was the product of over thirty years' reflection and propaganda and appeared on the third occasion that the issue of Euthanasia was brought before the House of Lords. The Bill is reproduced in the Appendix so that its provisions may be properly considered.

In the first clause of the Bill sub-section (2) the terms 'euthanasia', 'qualified patient' and 'irremediable condition' are defined.

The definition of euthanasia is 'the painless inducement of death'. This is merely a euphemistic phrase for painless killing.

A 'qualified patient' means one 'over the age of majority in respect of whom two physicians (one being of consultant status) have certified in writing that the patient appears to them to be suffering from an irremediable condition'. The age of majority is no longer the traditional twenty-one years but eighteen years, at which age voting, marriage and legal contracts may now be undertaken. The difference is not great in terms of time, but often significant in terms of outlook. What may appear unendurable in the late teens, may become tolerable and even acceptable a few years later. Examples readily come to mind, particularly the result of accident such as head injury, loss of a limb or of sight, or disfigurement by burns. These conditions are not infrequently associated with depression and severe distress, persisting for months or more than a year; yet later, life again becomes desirable. But the Bill could be made a ready death warrant for the impetuous young, depressed after a serious injury.

There is nothing in the definition of the 'qualified patient', or elsewhere in the Bill, requiring that he be of sound mind, or that his appreciation of his act be judged adequate (although this is touched upon in the attestations of the witnesses to the signing of the declaration). So, under the Bill, we ask our doctors to certify, perhaps years after the signing of the declaration, that the patient suffers an irremediable condition, thus becoming 'qualified', without regard to whether he is sane and thus able to appreciate his position or revoke his declaration.

'Irremediable condition' is defined as '*a serious physical illness or impairment* reasonably thought in the patient's case *to be incurable* and expected to cause him severe distress or render him *incapable of rational existence*' (our italics). Every one of these terms requires thought. The course of life impairs our resources. The course of life induces severe distress. It is far more common for the course of life to be attended by ailment than not, and for middle age to usher in that period when ailments crowd about us more easily and persist more readily. At first flush the term 'serious physical illness' conjures up pain, temperature, vomiting, cough and so on—in other words acute severe illness. In current medicine these conditions are often short lived and commonly are susceptible to treatment, so that these, commonly being regarded as curable, would not, occurring alone, lead to the implementation of euthanasia. A 'serious physical illness reasonably thought in the patient's case to be incurable and expected to cause him severe distress or render him incapable of rational existence', then, seems to exclude those acute severe illnesses mentioned above when these complicate an existing chronic illness.

As an example of the sort of condition presumably envisaged in the Bill, one could take coronary disease (disease of the arteries supplying blood to the heart muscle) with its attendant pain, occasional critical and severe episodes and progressive limitation of activity. It is particularly characteristic of this disease that marked distress and anxiety are associated with the bouts of pain or discomfort. From the onset of the condition until death, there may be a time interval of ten years or more. The last months may well find the patient, especially the elderly one, bed-ridden or nearly so. Between attacks of the illness the patient, though more limited in physical activity with the progress of the condition, is, typically, clear in mind. Let us assume he has signed his declaration (more than thirty days earlier) and is duly 'qualified'. According to his declaration (see the Schedule to the Bill in the Appendix) he is now free to indicate to his doctor the time or circumstances in which he is to be killed. Or (to continue with the schedule) if he becomes incapable of giving directions, then the discretion of the physician in charge of the case would become the deciding factor. Here no period of time or other qualification of such incapacity is indicated, so that it is presumably a matter of medical interpretation only, whether a transient episode of confusion in an elderly person with coronary disease or some other acute and otherwise curable illness would suffice for the physician to assume the discretion to act. This shows the grave discrepancy between the definition of a qualified patient in the Bill and the clear implications of the schedule and the declarations based on it.

If instead of chronic heart disease we consider chronic kidney disease, and remember the number of those who now, as opposed to a few years ago, can be maintained alive and in relative comfort by kidney machines at hospital and in their own homes, and then think of one of these patients requesting that he be despatched, the request is patently macabre.

The definition 'irremediable condition' quoted above also provides for a patient becoming 'incapable of rational existence', and the declaration as set out in the Schedule to the Bill repeats this and also mentions, as indicated above, the patient's becoming incapable of giving directions, as distinct from becoming incapable of rational existence. So it would appear, by virtue of the use of two forms of words, that 'incapable of rational existence' means a long-term condition whereas 'incapable of giving directions' could refer to a short term condition. The legal scrutiny of the Bill in chapter 5 has shown the unacceptability of the phrase 'incapable of rational existence', but the phrase 'incapable of giving directions' is relatively clear : it covers states of confusion (which may vary in intensity and be interrupted by lucid intervals), loss of speech due to brain damage, stroke, or tumour, and degenerative disease impairing comprehension such as senile or other forms of dementia. These are all regarded by practising physicians as physical illnesses and could be regarded as conforming to the criteria of causing severe distress or rendering incapable of rational existence. All the conditions mentioned above may be characterised by, or punctuated during their course by, episodes in which the patient is incapable of giving directions either by virtue of confusion or by loss of physical powers of expression. A physician is then burdened with the sole responsibility if and when to kill in such circumstances.

In the 1936 Bill there were provisions for relatives to object. There were no similar provisions in the 1969 Bill. Nonetheless it seems improbable that the attitude of the relatives could be ignored by the physician. Indeed, it could be argued that were the written consent of the close relatives not obtained, some awkward litigation might ensue from disappointed or outraged kinsfolk. If, in self-protection, the doctor required the written consent of available relatives, what effect would this have on these at the time and later? And what of relatives not available at that moment? How near must the relatives be in kinship—and how far must the net of consent be spread?

As a person approaches death along the path of illness, he commonly finds residual life the sweeter, or at any rate appears to wish more to cling to living. The Bill does not provide for or take account of likely consequences of this change. What is to happen when a patient incapable of giving directions nonetheless shows by other signs that he wishes to continue to live, yet the doctor is well aware that there exists a valid declaration, perhaps months or years old, in which the patient asserts that in circumstances like the present he wishes to be killed? In these circumstances the doctor is in the unenviable position of being apparently prevented by Statute Law from using his judgement freely in the clinical setting. The 1969 Bill at no point makes it clear that a given doctor is *bound* to implement his patient's instructions with regard to his euthanastic demise. By virtue of the conscience clause in the Bill, those who seek its protection would be exempt from implementing such euthanastic desires. What, however, would be the implications of a case like the following? A patient has become duly qualified and is under the care of the consultant and/or family doctor who signed the certificates. He is now in confusion owing, let us say, to a localised brain haemorrhage. The doctor does not kill him. He recovers enough to return to lucidity and finds that, in addition to the chronic disease from which he suffered, he is now partly paralysed. The doctor might have been expected to foresee the disability which would follow the stroke, yet has permitted his patient to survive. Would not the patient have grounds to lay a suit for damages against the doctor who has 'caused' him, by not killing him in his confused state, to suffer distress and disability (regardless of the grounds on which the doctor's decision was not to kill was based)?

In other words, is there not an *implicit undertaking on the part of the doctor* who knowingly accepts the care of a qualified patient to kill him either at the patient's instigation or if a condition supervene which might cause further deterioration? (Had the Bill passed, the law would have become uncertain on this point.)[1] Lest the hypothetical example quoted be considered ludicrous, it should be noted that in the United States of America cases have been brought against doctors for damages on behalf of deformed children who had been born alive because the doctor declined to carry out an abortion. The killing of patients is not the aim of the doctor or the nurse.

Now let us consider the term 'impairment': it must mean

---

[1] The scheme of the Bill is permissive: it does not set out to impose any statutory duty on a doctor to carry out euthanasia. It is unlikely that any statutory duty could be implied, but the possibility cannot be entirely excluded. A duty to a patient, or to an employer (a hospital authority), could probably only arise under express contract. There would be a breach of contractual duty if a doctor, having agreed to treat a patient, or agreed certain conditions of employment, subsequently refused to carry out euthanasia, either generally or in a particular case, unless the refusal could be shown to be founded on conscientious objection.

damage to, or loss of, structure or function of some part of the human body, including the brain, other parts of the nervous system and/or the mind. In this context, advanced age itself becomes an impairment, although a naturally occurring one, and is associated with impairments of various functions, from muscular strength and performance to breathing capacity and the functioning of the mind in its biochemical and nervous aspects. This is noticeable even when dementia is quite absent. These impairments may well cause severe distress and be quite incurable. Under such a heading as 'impairments expected to cause distress' may also come quite unexpected situations or conditions such as hysterectomy in a woman still yearning for a child or another child; the loss of sight or hearing, or of a limb. These constitute irremediable conditions within the meaning of the Bill. It is well known that all such conditions may be accompanied by the development of depressive mental illness, which may well induce the signing of a declaration, or the demand that one already signed be implemented. Such depressions may not respond at once to treatment and may well last longer than the thirty days stipulated in the Bill before a declaration asking for euthanasia was to become effective. The physician is thus in a cleft stick, knowing that an irremediable conditions exists, but that what leads to the demand for euthanasia is a curable illness which has come upon the patient. Yet for those who survive, life can again become sweet, even though the treatment of the depression (which may well have given rise to the desire for death) may itself have its own difficulties before a satisfactory outcome. Thus, from this aspect, the Bill would legalise the termination of life under the guise of a persisting impairment, when in fact the patient's desire for euthanasia stemmed from a depressive illness with a good prognosis.

No provision was made in the 1969 Bill for how long the irremediable condition should have endured before euthanasia could be implemented. Some irremediable conditions may go on for a very long period of time before inducing severe pain or distress or threatening rationality, and yet, in the terms of this Bill, anybody who had had such a condition diagnosed could quite clearly require that he be killed off before his distress become more than prospective.

One must remember that the duty of killing the patient may be delegated by the physician to the nurse. So the Bill asks doctors and nurses to kill another person at that person's behest. Furthermore they are asked to decide, if that patient become incapable of giving directions, to use professional judgement in lieu of the patient's indication. The implications of such a situation can only become nearly real if the reader actively imagines himself to be the nurse or doctor concerned, remembering the while that the symptoms of disease are largely, though not by any means entirely, capable of alleviation, so that acute severe distress and pain are not characteristic of chronic disease which is being actively treated. The doctor or nurse is being asked to kill instead of to give care and treatment. Is this a legitimate request to make of those who have devoted themselves to the care of the sick and dying, the preservation of health, and the treatment or cure of disease?

Thus doctors and nurses, especially those who sought to collaborate in this over-rational approach to dispensing death to another, would be in a self-contradictory situation, expecting themselves to observe one set of values with some of their patients and a contradictory set of values with others. Whether such doctors and nurses would be regarded by their patients as capable of observing any other than the destructive values is debatable, for it must be remembered that we are considering the outright killing of people by medical means, and not the easement of the pathway to death which is legitimate and current practice.

By Clause 4 of the Bill the physician in charge is required, in the case of a 'mentally responsible patient', to 'ascertain to his reasonable satisfaction that the declaration and all steps proposed to be taken under it accord with the patient's wishes'. (The term 'mentally responsible' has been scrutinised for its meaning in law in Chapter 5 and found wanting in precision. It could well be assumed to mean lucid or clear in mind, but this is not specified.) The Bill requires that 'the declaration and all steps to be taken under it . . . accord with the patient's wishes'. So the doctor is to satisfy himself that the patient (a) wishes to be killed even though, capable of rescinding his declaration, he has not done so and (b) *approves of the steps in the procedure* (our italics). The degree of detail is not specified, but the implication can hardly be escaped that the patient must assent to the pill, the preliminary and/or the fatal injection as the case may be. It is a scene which must be conjured up clearly if one is to appreciate its inherent inhumane qualities. The dead cannot speak and the physician alone bears the responsibility.

The question of onus of proof after the event, that the patient wished to be killed at the given time, was not settled in the Bill. One can imagine the furore of relatives wrangling over a Will and the delicate position in which a doctor could find himself unless he had a written, detailed consent, signed by the patient, specifying the time and mode of death, with which to confront the dispossessed who had hopes of a new Will being made. And the whole problem could be much more complex in the case of a confused, disoriented patient, or one who could no longer convey his wishes clearly, or one who could no longer write his name. It is of no help that the form of declaration must be signed and witnessed at least thirty days before killing. The fact that the witnesses declared on the form that the patient 'appeared to appreciate its significance' would not be relevant to the problems raised here, for clarity of mind in the chronic sick and specially the more elderly sick may alter very much in a month. A month is, in these conditions, a relatively long clinical period.

Clause 4 of the Bill refers to the administration of euthanasia to a mentally responsible patient: it is silent with regard to a patient who is not mentally responsible. The Schedule to the Bill however enables the witnesses to the declaration to testify that the 'declarant was unable to write but assented to this declaration in our presence, and appeared to appreciate its significance'. This statement could cover conditions in which the patient was sufficiently disturbed mentally (whether by virtue of physical disease of the brain or by virtue of other sorts of mental disease) to misapprehend the implication of the document and thus assent to it. How the patient is to indicate assent is not made clear in the schedule. It could be by word or gesture. Nor is there any indication of the grounds on which the witnesses decide to judge the appearances of appreciation of the significance of the declaration to the declarant. In one who could neither write nor speak or one who was gravely disturbed by brain damage or insanity, unconventional modes of indication of appreciation would have to be relied upon. The witnesses could well find themselves in an unenviable position if they were called upon to defend their judgement later. The peculiarly broad and loose phraseology of the testimony of the witnesses as set out in the schedule seems designed, no doubt by accident, to facilitate mistakes in the killing of patients. These, of course, would then be irretrievable, for the witnesses put their signatures to these words: 'We do not know of any pressure being brought on him to make a declaration and we believe it is made by his own wish'.

The above may be held to be a point of law and not related to medical matters, but in practice it is more than likely that were such a Bill to become law, doctors and nurses, especially in hospitals, would be asked to act as witnesses, for relatives must by definition or implication be excluded as they might well stand to benefit by the declarant's death. Those doctors and nurses would be unlikely to be so privy to the patient's private family life as to know whether the statements in their testimony regarding absence of pressure brought upon the patient were worth the paper they were written upon.

The considerations in the present and preceeding chapter have shown, it is hoped, that the concept of legalised killing of sick persons is not one that doctors and nurses should be expected to carry out and that, in the press of practice, neither doctors nor nurses, to whom the killing may be delegated, are in a good position to interpret either the principle or the terms of the late Bill. The principle is dubious if not damaging, and the terms, though appearing clear and meaningful, are much less than this when examined. It is not disputed that the proponents of the Bill seek to spare humans suffering. What is disputed is whether a legal instrument is the appropriate method. It is here claimed that the sparing of suffering has been the goal of medicine always. The proponents of euthanasia would give the impression that this is not so in regard to the chronic and incurable severe illnesses. In this they wrong the doctors and nurses who devote themselves to this sort of work. An argument is often put forward, that there is a certain amount of euthanasia practised at present in an unofficial capacity, and that this should be legalised. This argument arises from the confusion of the two meanings of the term euthanasia which have already been noticed. The Bill uses the term for the outright killing of a sick person at his behest or on the doctor's direct and intended initiative; the initial meaning of the term is a good and happy death or, in a phrase, the easement of the pathway to death. We maintain that the former does not in practice occur to any significant degree; doctors or nurses do not deliberately kill off patients. The initial, more traditional, meaning of euthanasia, however, a good and happy death, a quiet death, is in fact the aim of all medical care of terminal cases. This easement of the pathway to death, euthanasia in its original sense, is by no means, and must not be regarded as, the practice of killing the patient on the quiet.

Chapter X

A sample of medical attitudes

Nurses and doctors enjoy a privileged status in the community, which stems from the nature of their work : the relief of suffering and the preservation of life. On this, not only does their status in the community depend, but the function and role they fulfil and occupy in the minds of sick and well alike. We are properly outraged when we learn of maltreatment of the sick in hospital or the neglect of the sick and infirm at home or elsewhere, and our outrage is directed against the nurses and doctors who may have failed their role and responsibility, notwithstanding the contingent difficulties in which they may at the time be working. This is because, and only because, we as a society regard the sick as warranting special care and the nurses and doctors as our special agents for this care, who have selected themselves for this particular mode of life.

A questionnaire reproduced on page 120 in all essentials save those permitting identification, was sent by a member of the Medical Staff of a London Hospital to his seventy consultant colleagues. (The 1969 Bill required one of the certifying doctors to be of consultant status.) Fifty-six replies were received. This questionnaire was organised in order to supply data for a public debate on euthanasia. It was circulated before the enquirer knew of the contents of the 1968 Draft Bill : in its initial paragraph therefore it reflects the elaborate safeguards of the 1936 Bill. The 1968 Draft Bill, and Lord Raglan's Bill of 1969 did not require witnesses to the act of euthanasia, and did not make arrangements for a euthanasia referee, nor for the notification of relatives.

The consistency of opinion and attitude of the very great majority of those who replied is marked as one looks at the answers to the inter-related questions. As the replies to the questionnaire were not signed unless the respondent wished to declare himself, anonymity was preserved and the outcome may be regarded as unbiased. These consultants (of varying, if any, religious persuasion) are preponderantly against the killing of a patient, unofficially or officially (Questions 1–3 inclusive). Questions 4, 5 and 6 deal essentially with the easement of the pathway to death, and the respondents are preponderantly in favour of this: the patient's pain and distress should be relieved, even if this be likely to shorten life; treatment should, when it is merciful so to do, be withheld, and measures to relieve pain and mental distress of the dying should not be limited to those which would not be expected to shorten life.

Finally the consultants, on the whole, are satisfied with the present state of the law in so far as it touches on their care of the dying patient.

Thus the picture emerging is that experienced consultant physicians and surgeons and their colleagues in other specialities in the whole field of medicine do not consider that they are hampered by the law, as it is at present, in making the dying patient comfortable. They are prepared to accept the secondary, or side effect of shortening a dying person's life in the pursuit of his peace and comfort. But they do not accept the principle of desirability of actual killing of sick people for whom they care, whether officially sanctioned or carried out 'on the quiet'. Thus they support the traditional concept of euthanasia as a happy form of death, but not the meaning given it in the Bill.

It is recognised that a single large hospital does not necessarily provide an accurate sample of opinion and does not necessarily reflect opinion among consultants in other hospitals, nor does this investigation reveal the opinion of general practitioners or nurses. Nonetheless it is a sample of senior medical opinion from a hospital which has no religious affiliations and which is not remarkable for its conservatism of outlook.

It could be argued by some that the views of experienced physicians and surgeons regarding a topic such as euthanasia must be much influenced by the general climate of opinion of the society in which they live. In ours, euthanasia is yet far from acceptance, as the debates in the Lords and the defeat of Mr Gray's Motion in the Commons in April 1970 have shown. (See chapter IV.) This has also been shown by the fact that no public debate on this matter has produced a vote in favour of euthanasia. Nonetheless, it could be urged by some that if euthanasia were to be made lawful, the climate of general opinion would change so as to be more favourable, and the views of doctors would keep in step. All this is conjecture and out of keeping with the firm declaration against euthanasia made by the British Medical Association in 1969, and the Resolution passed at the AGM of that body in April 1970.

Nonetheless, even were such a change in climate of social opinion to occur, it is worth considering very gravely the change in values and attitudes which society would then be requiring of its nurses and doctors. This would be a bad change, from the values of the life-preserver to the life-depriver.

It is held that the replies to the questionnaire give no support to the idea that these doctors seek to prolong the process of dying at the cost of the distress, mental or physical, of their patients, and it is also held that this is a fair statement of the attitudes of doctors and nurses in general, and that the medical and nursing resources of the community are in essential opposition to the principle of killing those entrusted to their care.

QUESTIONNAIRE

The aims of the Euthanasia Society, in brief, are to legalise voluntary euthanasia by a single act aimed to terminate life under carefully defined conditions, e.g. in the presence of two witnesses, duly certified by a special euthanasia referee who checks the proposal personally, the relatives being duly informed and given the time and opportunity to object.

	Yes	No	No answer	Other, No opinion, or doubtful
1. Are you generally in favour of the Euthanasia Society's proposals?	4	50	0	2 no opinion
2. If not, would you favour legislation of euthanasia under different conditions?	1	48	4	1 '?', 2 no opinion
3. If you oppose legislation of voluntary euthanasia would you favour its application unofficially at the judgement only of the patient's medical practitioner?	0	47	6	1 'not sure' 2 no opinion
4. Do you agree that relief of pain and mental distress of a patient believed to be dying should be achieved even if the measures are likely to shorten the patient's life?	52	1	0	1 'possible yes' 2 no opinion

	Yes	No	No answer	Other, No opinion, or doubtful
5. Should treatment of a dying patient some-times be withheld if shortening his life was thought merciful?	53	0	0	1 'sometimes' 2 no opinion
6. Do you think that measures to relieve pain and mental distress of a patient believed to be dying should be limited to those which are not expected to shorten the patient's life span?	1	53	0	2 no opinion
7. Are you generally satisfied with the present state of the law insofar as it may influence your care of the dying patient?	47	4	2	1 '?' 2 no opinion

Chapter XI

Euthanasia, the family, and society

The advocates of euthanasia say they seek to reduce the amount of suffering among the aged and infirm or others in terminal distress. Although their arguments are couched in terms of compassion for the dying, the problem cannot be considered in terms of the dying person alone, for the relatives and friends of each dying person are intimately associated with the death. And not they only: the care and treatment of the dying—as indeed of other patients—is ultimately the concern of the whole of society. The culture of the society in which they have lived has determined the attitudes of the patient, the relatives and the medical attendants; their conduct springs from and in its turn reacts upon that culture and thus finally upon the whole of society.

Let us consider first the sick man or woman. A sick person's reaction to pain depends on physical, psychological and cultural factors. Physically, the level at which pain becomes agonising varies greatly between individuals, so that pain which for one man is well within the threshold of tolerance, is to another unendurable. Psychologically, suffering caused by comparatively slight causes may be built up to an intolerable degree by neurotic fears. Culturally, a patient who regards pain as utterly negative and to be relieved by all possible means will not exert himself to come to terms with it, and will thus appear to have a very low threshold of toleration. If, on the other hand, he regards pain as a natural part of his condition, and his condition as the common lot of man, the enduring of pain will be to him one of the ordinary difficulties of life—and, he will expect, of death. Accepting pain in this way is quite common among ordinary people: it does not require superhuman courage nor heroic virtue. The heroic approach to pain is something unknown to most people, and incomprehensible to many of those who have heard of it.

Among Christians the ideal is to be able consciously and prayerfully to offer up their suffering in union with the Passion of Christ; a few of the greatest are even able to welcome a painful death as an opportunity to do this. However, this is exceptional and it is quite wrong to suppose, as some appear to do, that Christians regard pain in general as a good thing *because* it provides such an opportunity. It is an affliction of which good use can often be made.

When death approaches, the cultural determinants in the patient's attitude to his suffering become predominant. To our ordinary human nature the approach of death is a fearful thing; this fear can be overcome at least in great part either by resignation or by hope. For those who deem there is no future after death, resignation to the inevitable must be the only way to grapple with the fear of death. To those on the other hand who are persuaded of the immortality of the soul, death, while remaining awesome, is seen as the portal to the future. It cannot but remain awesome, for the change of state which it involves is beyond the grasp of our imagination. What is essential at the approach of death is that the patient should be mentally composed to accept it. Patients will not be so composed if they feel that it may be brought to them unexpectedly early, or that they are under pressure to seek it out.

If voluntary euthanasia were to be legalised, would not many a dying person be in just such a position? If he had expressed a wish to be put away *in extremis*, he could be in two minds whether to withdraw his request; if he had never expressed such a wish he might feel that those about him would be relieved if he were to do so. This brings us directly to the consideration of the relatives and their role at the deathbed. The family is the primary unit in which human love is expressed and experienced, however imperfectly in practice. It is first of all the unit in which, and by means of which, human love is expressed in terms of life, in that the parents' love for each other is expressed procreatively. Their capacity for love is further expressed in the rearing of their children, and the responsive love of the children for their parents is the parents' fundamental source of security in the dependency of old age. On the basis of secure love, family bonds and loyalty are nurtured, and mutual devotion develops between the members of the family. Thus children who grow up in an atmosphere of love and security become aware of their own individuality, of the dignity of others, and of the needs, rights and duties of all. Where the sense of belonging, of community, exists, there is a rallying of forces for mutual support if the family meets with misfortune. In helping each other the members of the family find the family bonds strengthened. It is true that there are many families among whom this picture of family life, love and loyalty, may ring hollow. Yet it is not an idealised picture: on the contrary it is the picture of a wholesome, natural family.

The relationship of a dying person to his kith and kin has to be considered first in the normal family as described above, and secondly, in the family in which love, loyalty and mutual concern have not developed—in other words, the 'flawed family'. In the normal family, even if euthanasia were to be legalised, it is doubtful if the dying grandparent would express a wish for euthanasia or would think that his children and grandchildren wished that he might do so. In the flawed family, on the contrary, if the dying grandparent had not expressed a wish for euthanasia he might well be asking himself, 'These children and grandchildren around my bed, are they wishing in their hearts that I would ask for euthanasia?' Now, he cannot know whether they are wishing that or not; he may imagine they are when they are not; for their part they may find that thought in their hearts, but succeed in repressing it. A difficulty arises here, for if the members of the family are half wishing that the old man would ask for euthanasia so that they could be rid of him, outward courtesy may not prevent their feeling getting through to the dying man. Imagine his agony in such a case! In the confusion of human emotions, who could hope to arrive at a rational decision as to what exactly was to be done? It may be that in a more seriously flawed family the children and grandchildren would not even bother to gather round the bed of their dying grandparent, who would thus suffer a lonely death. Loneliness is a well known cause of suicide : the closeness of the comparison is disquieting. Inevitably, and particularly in the flawed family, the moment euthanasia was legalised there would be pressure, even if not overt, upon some patients to ask for it—to sign whatever form the law prescribed as their death warrant. Thus although described as voluntary, euthanasia would be requested under pressure in many cases, from the very beginning.

The patient would not be the only one to suffer from this unhappy situation. It is not difficult to imagine the guilty feelings which would arise among the members of a family, or the possibility—indeed virtual certainty—of dissension between them, and the increase in stress which that would cause. These results would be harmful to every member of the family, but probably most especially they would be damaging to children in their formative years. The long-term psychological consequences for that family are daunting. Each one of those who assented to the death has to come to his own death bed.

When one is considering the effect on a family of the implementation of legalised voluntary euthanasia one is apt to assume that an old person would be the sufferer, but irremediable conditions can affect all age-groups. When a young person is so affected, either as the aftermath of an acute illness or in the course of a progressive deterioration, he may well remain cheerful, well supported by his family and friends, either at home or in hospital if skilled care is required. A certain youthful optimism persists, a sense of achievement in overcoming difficulties, and the question of euthanasia would be most unlikely to occur to him —unless presented from outside. Nor would such a young adult, in health, prior to being incapacitated, be likely to have made the sort of declaration that is proposed. Such is the optimism of youth that the idea that 'this could never happen to me' would probably pertain. In the somewhat unlikely event of a young person becoming a 'qualified patient', one can imagine frantic efforts by him and his family to reverse the process. Even in a family where the bonds of affection are weak, parents and siblings would not view with equanimity the implementation of a death wish by a young man or woman.

One category of possible client is essentially a product of our times—the confirmed drug addict. We learn that there are now two thousand known addicts in the U.K. of whom about eight hundred are under twenty years of age. According to Home Office statistics, in 1972 the number may well have risen to ten thousand, approximately one in every three being a teenager. By the time a person has become addicted to 'hard' drugs, with or without the added horror of intravenous self-administration of barbiturates, the condition could be said to be irremediable with a hopeless prognosis and much reduced life expectancy—such people seldom reach thirty years of age. They are usually very well aware of the hopelessness of their condition, their degradation, physical deterioration and susceptibility to infection of all kinds. Whereas in the early days of drug experimentation rehabilitation is always a possibility to be tried and tried again, the confirmed addict is out of reach. Were voluntary euthanasia to be legalised one can conjure up a horrific state of affairs where young people, inextricably caught up in drug pushing, could be dispatched at their own request at some point in time. Self reproach and guilt feelings, already prevalent among the families of drug addicts, would certainly be intensified if such became the pattern.

If one considers the case of a mature person, say the father of a family, who had become a 'qualified patient', what would be the reactions in his family? If he had chosen to keep his intention secret one could imagine the resultant incredulity among those nearest and dearest to him. Even if the decision had been taken after careful reflection and full discussion with his spouse, one does not need much imagination to spell out the anxieties that would crowd in when the end appeared imminent.

From these considerations it is clear that it is absurd to regard a man's decision to ask for euthanasia as a matter that concerns him alone, and one that he can choose freely. Over three and a half centuries ago John Donne wrote : 'No man is an Iland, intire of itselfe . . . any man's death diminishes me because I am involved in Mankinde.' This is as true today as when it was first written.

We have maintained that genuinely voluntary euthanasia is impossible among those living in family circumstances. What of society as a whole? Those who no longer live in a family—the elderly, the childless, or those whose descendants and other relatives are far away, or have pre-deceased them—have to fall back on the care of the society of which their family was a part. For not only is the family the primary unit of human life and love, it is also a basic unit of society at large. What we have and are is part and parcel of the race and nation to which we belong. It is true that few of us normally think in these terms : but in Europe anyway (not of course in America) the nation is a historical extension of a group of tribes, so that the nation is in a very real sense an extension of the family. One of the traditions of our race and nation—as indeed of most peoples—is that we care for the old and infirm and do not take our aged grandparents out into the wilds and leave them to die. The aged and infirm then, who have no family upon whom to lean, ought to be able to expect the same sort of care from society as their more fortunate brothers and sisters expect from their children and kinsfolk.

Yet one can see how such care could be lacking. The family is small, coherent; each member means something to the other members. Society is large, impersonal. In a nation of many millions one individual old person is in danger of becoming a negligible statistic—except among those who feel a calling to serve the old. Society as a whole, careless as most people may be about the problem of geriatric care, nevertheless wishes old people to be able to pass their declining years contentedly. If euthanasia were legalised, the elderly could no longer feel this protection. Even though it were still left to the individual to decide whether or not he should opt for the morbid release, geriatric cases would inevitably fall into two classes—those who had and those who had not so opted. In the current controversy, the inadequate physical capacity of geriatric homes and hospitals has been mentioned by the proponents of euthanasia as if it were a fact in favour of their arguments. It is on the contrary irrelevant: if society does not wish euthanasia on other grounds, shortage of geriatric hospitals is no adequate ground for proposing it. Nevertheless, if euthanasia were to be legalised in circumstances of a shortage of geriatric capacity, it is not difficult to foresee what would happen. A few hospitals, staffed by those genuninely devoted to the care of the elderly and dying, would continue their work undeterred, but others, faced with a constant shortage of beds, would almost inevitably begin to prefer among prospective entrants those who had already agreed that in certain circumstances they should be killed. Gruesome as it sounds, such hospitals would, almost before they realised what they were doing, be ceasing to rate their achievement in terms of the contentment in life and the calm acceptance of death by their patients, and be beginning to rate it in terms of turnover.

In considering the hidden pressures which would arise between the patient and his relatives, and in considering the likely reaction of the practice of euthanasia on the conduct of geriatric hospitals, one is forced to the conclusion that, were voluntary euthanasia to be legalised, the voluntary aspect would soon be lost.

Once it has been declared that a man has a right to die if he feels that society cannot support him, or that his relatives wish him away, there would then be few grounds on which to resist the extension of the principle to euthanasia 'in the public interest'—economically or even genetically. Among the proponents of euthanasia the argument has commonly been heard that if an animal in suffering is put down as an act of mercy, it is a greater act of mercy to put down a suffering human being. Yet sick dogs or wounded horses cannot sign declarations requesting euthanasia. So much for the voluntary principle! Thus even before voluntary euthanasia is accepted, the voluntary nature of it is set aside by its own supporters.

To the individual dying man or woman, euthanasia would bring added anxieties. To the relatives it would bring intolerable stress. To society at large a step commended as granting private control of the right to die would inevitably become the first step towards state control of the right to life.

Chapter XII

Conclusion

From the detailed examination of the various aspects of the question in the preceding chapters, it has become apparent that the propaganda in favour of voluntary euthanasia has been based on a series of misconceptions. It is now time to state these misconceptions clearly, to show in their place the true conceptions, thus restating the positive arguments against voluntary euthanasia.

The first misconception is that doctors are under a legal and ethical obligation to keep people alive to the uttermost of their ability in all circumstances. This is repeated several times in the book *Euthanasia and the Right to Death*.[1] Oft repetition however does not alter the fact that this idea of the doctors' ethical and legal duty is quite simply untrue. It is true, unfortunately, that some doctors sometimes act as if they were under some sort of duty of this kind: the medical profession is well aware that some doctors enter the profession with an inadequate understanding of medical ethics. Important work is being done to overcome this by, for example, the Institute of Religion and Medicine and

---

[1] For example: 'We have to remember that, as the law stands at present, if he [i.e. the doctor] does not do all he can to preserve the tortured life up to the last possible gasp, he renders himself liable to grave penalties—even perhaps to the charge of murder', page 28 (W. R. Matthews).
And again: 'The sufferer may be reduced to an obscene parody of a human being. . . . This, as things now stand, must persist until at last every device of medical skill fails to prolong the horror', page 33 (Anthony Flew).
Such remarks can only be described as an 'obscene parody' of the present state of the law and of medical practice. (See the words of Mr Justice Devlin quoted on page 70.)

the London Medical Group.[2] The truth on this point is that although doctors properly strive to save the life of a seriously sick or injured person, they accept—and so does the law—that death is the natural end of life, and that where there is no prospect of a patient's life, and his enjoyment of life, being preserved for an appreciable period of time, the doctor will not and should not heap one procedure upon another for the sake of preserving a semblance of life. While nature can be assisted to preserve life in the psychosomatic structure which is man, the doctor will give that assistance: when nature turns her back on such assistance the prudent doctor, though he may coax her gently, will not attempt to force her against her better judgement.

The second misconception that must be corrected is that which states that a certain amount of euthanasia is already practised by doctors. The foregoing chapters have discussed this from the ethical and practical point of view, and have considered the legal implications of the ethically acceptable practice of administering pain-killing drugs in sufficient doses to achieve their purpose even if incidentally life is thereby shortened. It is probably from a misunderstanding of this practice that this particular misconception springs. For example, if a doctor says to a patient's relatives 'I will do what I can', and then administers a drug in a more liberal dosage than he has been using theretofore and the patient dies a few hours later, the relatives may—and many doctors have had experience of this—nod their heads sagely, clearly indicating that they have put two and two together and 'know' that the doctor has put his patient to death. In such circumstances it is useless for the doctor to explain his action in detail to them, for they will merely assume that he is excusing himself. This is an annoying and embarrassing experience for a doctor. Nevertheless, he knows in his own mind and conscience that his patient has died from the sickness which he was suffering, and not from a deliberate overdose of a drug.

Thirdly, there is the misconception as to the amount of intractable pain that still surrounds death. Much pain undoubtedly there frequently is: but intractable pain is a different matter.

[2] Referred to by the Bishop of Durham in the 1969 Debate: Hansard, H. of L., vol 300, col 1185.

Even in his time Dr Millard seems to have taken too gloomy a view of the problem, and whereas he pessimistically forecast that the proportion of very painful deaths would increase, thanks to the advances in medical science the proportion has steadily dropped, and continues to do so. In fact now no one in medical care need die in agony.

More confused thinking is introduced into the discussion by the term 'the right to death'. The argument seems to be that if there is a right to life this must be balanced by a comparable right to death. Yet how can this be? Civilised society safeguards for each of its citizens (except perhaps those guilty of serious crimes) the right to life. That right is acknowledged by human law givers, but it was not invented by them; it springs from man's nature. Nor is it a political right like the franchise which can be granted or withheld according to the type of constitution. It is an absolute right: though certain individuals may forfeit it, e.g. by crime, no individual can renounce it either for himself or for others.

The term 'right to death' is, moreover, a euphemism. It is true that since the Suicide Act of 1961 anyone is free to attempt *felo-de-se* without being in peril of the law, but what is meant by the right to death in the context of euthanasia is far more than the right to commit *felo-de-se*. In this context the right to death involves other people acting as accessories, namely doctors and nurses. Thus the so-called right to death is not simply the right of a man to kill himself. It means the right to be put to death, and necessarily involves the right of others to kill.

Still more confusion is added by frequent reference to 'the quality rather than the quantity of life'. Just what is meant by the term 'the quality of life' is not clear. What is abundantly clear is that such quality as a life has while it persists is expunged when it ceases. That is to say, it is impossible for death to improve the quality of life. The only possible way in which the death of an individual can be said to enhance the quality of life is statistically: the elimination of the lower quality lives would leave the survivors showing a higher average quality of life. This is the principle upon which we cull our flocks and herds. There are those who consider the human 'herd' should be culled in the same way. The Voluntary Euthanasia Society as a body would certainly not be in favour of such drastic measures, but the introduction of this term 'quality of life' makes one wonder whether the members of that Society are clear in their own minds as to the direction in which their propaganda is tending.

In analysing the arguments used in the euthanasia controversy one is struck by the number of deeply distressing examples that are quoted by supporters of euthanasia which would not have been covered by any of the Bills so far produced. One such heart-rending case was featured by the BBC in October 1969.[3] A boy who had been very seriously injured at the age of sixteen was resuscitated from a very low state, to lie for six months in a coma. Eventually he recovered consciousness but is likely to spend the rest of his life in a hospital or institution, being largely paralysed and speaking only with difficulty. The Commentator's last words on that programme were: 'One mother's deep, emotional and moving argument for euthanasia.' Now that lad would not have been eligible for voluntary euthanasia because he was under the age of majority. One may say that his doctors were unwise in persisting in resuscitation in that particular case—it is so easy to be wise after the event—but if the doctors had made the contrary decision, that is had not persisted in resuscitation and had allowed the patient to die, this would *not* have been euthanasia. If the 1969 Bill had become law that case, clearly presented as an argument for euthanasia, would not have been affected in any way by it. Only four days later euthanasia was again mentioned in a broadcast, this time on television.[4] The subject under discussion was spina bifida, and the question was raised as to whether suffering infants should be allowed to die. The doctor being interviewed explained the ethical principles simply and clearly, not disguising the practical difficulties sometimes involved in observing them. But as the programme concerned only infants, once again voluntary euthanasia was quite irrelevant.

It is extremely difficult for the mass media to present a controversial matter like euthanasia in a way which will satisfy

[3] Radio 4, 6 November 1969, 'The World at One'.
[4] ITV, 10 November 1969, 'Today'.

people of all opinions that it is free from bias. In this country happily one can be confident that programme producers are motivated by a sense of responsibility and wish to present a balanced picture. Their efforts are frequently successful.[5] Unfortunately however a true balance is not always maintained. Slipshod use of words can easily give a false impression. One difficulty is that producers and interviewers cannot be expected to have detailed knowledge of all the subjects with which they deal. They have the duty, and they have also the skill, to attract and hold viewers' and listeners' attention. In order to heighten the human interest they may appeal to the emotions of the audience, and this may be reflected in a varied emphasis on different facts or aspects of the matter. The upshot is that a programme, so far from being balanced, can become slanted, even when this is far from the intention of the producer or interviewer. At times this has happened. If the interviewer himself is prejudiced (by which is meant, holding an opinion on little or no evidence) the imbalance of the presentation can reach serious proportions.

There may well be many people who say they support the principle of voluntary euthanasia, but who have in mind types of cases which would not come into that category: how many of such people would be prepared to support euthanasia if the voluntary aspect were dropped? Some certainly would: Lord Chorley's remark, quoted on page 36, seems to indicate that he at least is aware of this. In the 1969 Lords Debate, Lord Ritchie-Calder in the course of his speech referred to briefly on page 60, made it clear that his pity extended not so much to the aunt who had been helpless from the age of two but to her sisters who had spent their lives looking after her. 'I could not' he said '. . . feel that two lives should be sacrificed for one.' He had previously said 'I was influenced by considerations which go far beyond the intentions of this Bill.' In the face of such remarks from those who have supported a voluntary euthanasia bill with voice and vote, it is hard for the supporters of voluntary euthanasia to pretend that their proposed legislation is motivated solely by pity for

[5] For example the programme in which Dr Gray and Mr St John-Stevas discussed the question with Bob Friend (Radio 4, 7 April 1970, 'Today').

the sufferers, or to dismiss as scaremongering the suggestion that voluntary euthanasia would be the thin end of the wedge. Thus the confusion of the argument is made worse confounded by the adherence to the cause of voluntary euthanasia of many who do not understand what it is and how restricted it must be if it is to be made legal, and of those who would prefer euthanasia not to be voluntary, but are prepared to support a voluntary euthanasia bill as a first step.

Much has been said in the course of this book of the weakness of the voluntary principle upon which the Euthanasia Society proposes that legislation should be based. It has been shown how extremely difficult it would be to ensure true consent at all necessary stages; how impossible it would be for a doctor to judge the presence or absence of consent in a patient unable to communicate for any reason; how easily hidden, subtle and perhaps quite unintentional pressures could influence a patient's decision to ask for euthanasia; how readily any defects in the working of a Euthanasia Act could lead to a watering down of the voluntary principle. The absence of safeguards to avoid such deep pitfalls would make a Euthanasia Act unthinkable. but study of the problem reveals that adequate safeguards would be so complex as to be unworkable. The legal and parliamentary experts of the Voluntary Euthanasia Society will doubtless continue to redraft their proposed legislation, and further attempts will doubtless be made to introduce a bill into Parliament. It is time for the general public to become aware of the underlying flaw : the principle of euthanasia is so radically unsound that it is bound to be impossible to draft sound legislation to enact it. Ill cannot be well done.

Appendix

The following is the text of the Bill introduced by Lord Raglan into the House of Lords in March, 1969, and rejected on Second Reading.

Voluntary Euthanasia Bill [H.L.]

EXPLANATORY MEMORANDUM

General

The main purpose of the Bill is to authorise physicians to give euthanasia to a patient who is thought on reasonable grounds to be suffering from an irremediable physical condition of a distressing character, and who has, not less than 30 days previously, made a declaration requesting the administration of euthanasia in certain specified circumstances one or more of which has eventuated.

Clause 1 provides that a physician may administer euthanasia to a 'qualified patient' who has made a declaration in the form set out in the schedule. A qualified patient is defined as a patient over the age of majority who has been certified by two physicians, one being of consultant status, to be apparently suffering from an irremediable condition. Subsection (2) defines the expressions used in the Bill.

Clause 2 provides that a declaration shall come into force 30 days after being made, and shall remain in force for three years. A declaration re-executed within 12 months preceding its expiry date shall remain in force for life, unless revoked.

Clause 3 provides that a declaration may be revoked at any time.

Clause 4 provides that before euthanasia may be given to a mentally responsible patient the physician in charge must ascertain to the best of his ability that the declaration and steps proposed to be taken under it accord with the patient's wishes. Subsection (2) provides that a nurse, acting on the directions of a physician, may cause euthanasia to be administered to a patient, and subsection (3) provides that no physician or nurse who is opposed on principle to euthanasia shall be required to take any steps in its administration.

Clause 5 protects physicians and nurses who act in good faith in the belief that their actions are in accordance with a patient's declaration or further requests made under the Act and provides that they shall not be in breach of any professional oath by administering euthanasia.

Clause 6 provides that a person who conceals, destroys, falsifies or forges a declaration commits an offence punishable by life imprisonment, and that an attesting witness who wilfully makes a false statement commits an offence punishable by up to 7 years' imprisonment.

Clause 7 provides that euthanasia shall not, except in limited circumstances, invalidate any insurance policy.

Clause 8 declares that all terminal patients are entitled to receive whatever quantity of drugs may be required to keep them entirely free from pain; and that in a case where severe distress cannot be alleviated by pain-killing drugs, the patient is entitled, if he so desires, to be made and kept entirely unconscious. The section applies to patients whether or not they have made any declaration, and is expressed to be for the removal of doubt as to the existing state of the law.

Clause 9 provides for the Secretary of State for Social Services to make regulations specifying classes of persons entitled or not entitled to witness a declaration, defining the duties of hospital physicians having responsibility for patients in relation to euthanasia, regulating the custody of declarations, and for any other purpose.

Clause 10 contains the short title and extent of the Act.

ARRANGEMENT OF CLAUSES

A
BILL
INTITULED

1969   An Act to provide in certain circumstances for the administration of euthanasia to persons who request it and who are suffering from an irremediable condition, and to enable persons to request in advance the administration of euthanasia in the event of their suffering from such a condition at a future date.

Be it enacted by the Queen's most Excellent Majesty, by and with the consent of the Lords Spiritual and Temporal, and Commons, in this present Parliament assembled, and by the authority of the same, as follows :

Authorisation of euthanasia.

1. (1) Subject to the provisions of this Act, it shall be lawful for a physician to administer euthanasia to a qualified patient who has made a declaration that is for the time being in force.

(2) For the purposes of this Act :

'physician' means a registered medical practitioner; 'euthanasia' means the painless inducement of death; 'qualified patient' means a patient over the age of majority in respect of whom two physicians (one being of consultant status) have certified in writing that the patient appears to them to be suffering from an irremediable condition;

'irremediable condition' means a serious physical illness or impairment reasonably thought in the patient's case to be incurable and expected to cause him severe distress or render him incapable of rational existence;

139

'declaration' means a witnessed declaration in writing made substantially in the form set out in the schedule to this Act.

Declaration made in advance.

2. (1) Subject to the provisions of this section, a declaration shall come into force 30 days after being made and shall remain in force (unless revoked) for three years.

(2) A declaration re-executed within the 12 months preceding its expiry date shall remain in force (unless revoked) during the lifetime of the declarant.

Mode of revocation.

3. (1) A declarant may be revoked at any time by destruction or by notice of cancellation shown on its face, effected (in either case) by the declarant or to his order.

Duties and rights of physicians and nurses.

4. (1) Before causing euthanasia to be administered to a mentally responsible patient the physician in charge shall ascertain to his reasonable satisfaction that the declaration and all steps proposed to be taken under it accord with the patient's wishes.

(2) Euthanasia shall be deemed to be administered by a physician if treatment prescribed by a physician is given to the patient by a state registered or state enrolled nurse.

(3) No person shall be under any duty, whether by contract or by any statutory or other legal requirement, to participate in any treatment Authorised by this Act to which he has a conscientious objection.

Protection for physicians and nurses.

5. (1) A physician or nurse who, acting in good faith, causes euthanasia to be administered to a qualified patient in accordance with what the person so acting believes to be the patient's declaration and wishes shall not be guilty of any offence.

(2) Physicians and nurses who have taken part in the administration of euthanasia shall be deemed not to be in breach of any professional oath or affirmation.

Offences.

6. (1) It shall be an offence punishable on indictment by a sentence of life imprisonment wilfully to conceal, destroy, falsify or forge a declaration with intent to create a false impression of another person's wishes with regard to euthanasia.

(2) A person signing a declaration by way of attestation who wilfully puts his signature to a statement he knows to be false shall be deemed to have committed an offence under section 2 of the Perjury Act 1911.

1911 c. 6.

Insurance policies.

7. No policy of insurance that has been in force for 12 months shall be vitiated by the administration of euthanasia to the insured.

Administration of drugs to patients suffering severe distress.

8. For the removal of doubt it is declared that a patient suffering from an irremediable condition reasonably thought in his case to be terminal shall be entitled to the administration of whatever quantity of drugs may be required to keep him free from pain, and such a patient in whose case severe distress cannot be otherwise relieved shall, if he so requests, be entitled to drugs rendering him continuously unconscious.

Power to make regulations.

9. (1) The Secretary of State for Social Services shall make regulations under this Act by statutory instrument for determining classes of persons who may or may not sign a declaration by way of attestation, for regulating the custody of declarations, for appointing (with their consent) hospital physicians having responsibility in relation to patients who have made or wish to make a declaration, and for the prescribing of any matters

he may think fit to prescribe for the purposes of this Act.

(2) Any statutory instrument made under this Act shall be subject to annulment in pursuance of a resolution of either House of Parliament.

Short title and extent. 10. (1) This Act may be cited as the Voluntary Euthanasia Act 1969.

(2) This Act does not extend to Northern Ireland.

SCHEDULE

Form of Declaration under The Voluntary Euthanasia Act 1969

Declaration made   19   [and re-executed
                          19   ]

by

of

I DECLARE that I subscribe to the code set out under the following articles :—

A. If I should at any time suffer from a serious physical illness or impairment reasonably thought in my case to be incurable and expected to cause me severe distress or render me incapable of rational existence, I request the administration of euthanasia at a time or in circumstances to be indicated or specified by me or, if it is apparent that I have become incapable of giving directions, at the discretion of the physician in charge of my case.

B. In the event of my suffering from any of the conditions specified above, I request that no active steps should be taken, and in particular that no resuscitatory techniques should be used, to prolong my life or restore me to consciousness.

C. This declaration is to remain in force unless I revoke it, which I may do at any time, and any request I may make concerning action to be taken or withheld in connection with this declaration will be made without further formalities

I WISH it to be understood that I have confidence in the good faith of my relatives and physicians, and fear degeneration and indignity far more than I fear premature death. I ask and authorise the physician in charge of my case to bear these statements in mind when considering what my wishes would be in any uncertain situation.

SIGNED

[SIGNED ON RE-EXECUTION]

WE TESTIFY that the above-named declarant* [signed] *[was unable to write but assented to] this declaration in our presence, and appeared to appreciate its significance. We do not know of any pressure being brought on him to make a declaration, and we believe it is made by his own wish. So far as we are aware, we are entitled to attest this declaration and do not stand to benefit by the death of the declarant.

Signed by   Signed by

of   of

[Signed by   [Signed by

of   of

on re-execution]   on re-execution]

* Strike out whichever words do not apply.